Enlightenment

Plain and Simple

Processes to Heal

Mind, Body, and Spirit.

A Path to

Enlightenment.

Enlightenment

Plain and Simple

Processes to Heal

Mind, Body, and Spirit.

By

Dean Graves

A path to Enlightenment.

Prema Healing

Meditation · Emotion Processing · Mindfulness

Copyright 2012 by Dean Graves

Published by

Prema Healing Meditation
159 N. White Station Road
Memphis, TN 38117
http://premameditation.com
info@premameditation.com

Cover and book design, editing, and type by
Prema Healing Meditation.

ISBN-13: 978-0615735900 (Prema Healing Meditation)

ISBN-10: 0615735908

According to Mandukya Upanishad ;

"enlightenment is a state of freedom from the ignorance that causes suffering. There is no necessity to attain mere belief in God, but it is necessary to have profound knowledge of the truth which lies behind the concept of the word God. The idea is not to know God as a different being but to know one's own real self and its essential nature, which is the self of all. The preaching(s) of religion make a person dependent on priests, temples, idols, blind faith and dogma and dependence on these is a habit of the lower mind. Such crutches may be useful at a certain stage for some people, but they do not lead one to ultimate truth. A dependent mind is not free, and without freedom, enlightenment is impossible. Religious dogmas are full of beliefs and myths that do not satisfy the human intellect and that bind believers to a narrow view of life and human potential. Such preaching(s) instill more fear than love in the hearts of masses".

Contents

Preface

Humanity has remained stuck in woefully low ranges of consciousness for far too long, and while significant effort is being made to assist mankind to raise the level of collective and individual consciousness, the actual work must be undertaken by each individual on an individual basis. The work is tedious at times and challenging at others, but it is work that must be done in order to move forward. This book and the tools within are just such efforts to assist mankind in moving forward.

Behavior is determined by consciousness. Consciousness is not determined by behavior. In order to improve the behavior of each individual person and the collective behavior of humanity it is necessary to raise the individual and collective consciousness of the planet. While this may seem to be a Herculean task, it is one that is achievable and with faster and longer lasting (forever) results than any conventional war, war on drugs, war on poverty, war on crime, etc.

If you want to change the world, change yourself. How you change yourself is to learn to have love and compassion for yourself and heal the wounds of battle that you have been fighting for multiple lifetimes. You will still need to be a warrior, but a peaceful warrior and with the results of your battles to be everlasting peace, both inward and outward.

The question you must ask yourself is, "Do I have the strength to heal? Do I have the strength to look inside and get to know myself? Is the pain of staying the same now greater than the pain of change?"

The methods and practices offered in this book are the simplest, most efficient, painless, and effective methods to be found anywhere. There are no pills that will do it for you. No one can perform a magic ceremony that will do it for you. Only you can heal you, because only you know how you made you sick.

Besides healing you will get to know your best friend in all of the world, your Higher Self. You will never be lonely, lost, forlorn, or friendless again. Like all of us, to date you have been exploring the dark cave of life without a flashlight. With the tools provided in this book you now have the brightest flashlight and the keys to the castle.

Do yourself a great service and come in from the darkness and heal yourself.

Introduction

The journey began for me about ten years ago. At the time my wife suffered from a chronic condition called Cluster Headaches. She had endured these since she was about fourteen years old and had learned to incorporate them into her life pretty well, maintaining a successful career and generally enjoying life in between the appearance of the headache cycles.

Approximately eleven or twelve years ago the cycle of headaches that she had learned to manage became chronic and were with her all of the time. She became completely unable to function and western medicine was unable to provide any reasonable solutions. Pain medicine became ineffective and massive doses of steroids were destroying her vital organs and eventually caused a total failure of her adrenal glands. In addition to the headaches she was totally exhausted all of the time and other life threatening conditions manifested as a result of the maintenance diet of steroids and pain medication.

She became addicted to the pain medications, fearful of not having them immediately available on demand at the outset of any hint of a headache symptom. Her time was spent in bed and often times in deep depression. It was not a happy time for either one of us. Still, we were confident that some resolution of the physical ailments could be found.

A relative of mine, a chiropractor, suggested an alternative treatment that was definitely unconventional. The treatment was not one that he could administer but referred us to a source where we could obtain treatment. It was a relative early form of emotional processing. Desperate to find a solution we tried it, and like the typical dutiful and protective husband I pushed her out in front and said, "Here, you try it."

The results were amazing. Remember I said that the method was an early method that was clumsy compared to more recent refinements, but in approximately 30 hours of processing the headaches went away and never returned. Most of the other physical ailments caused by the massive chemical treatments offered to try and stem the headache onslaught persisted however. She was still very sick, but the root cause of the ailments had been alleviated.

Something else occurred at the same time. She had a dramatic spiritual awakening. She became enlightened to a very high degree, and we later found out, reached the highest level of consciousness available to humanity. It was amazing the clarity that she had and things that she intuitively knew. To say the least, I was massively envious.

Regrettably, the consciousness lasted for only six to eight weeks and as she described it, she "fell back down the mountain". Even though her consciousness level returned to earlier levels and she still suffered from significant physical ailments, the cluster headaches didn't return. We both had been exposed to a tool that we both needed more of and had unknowingly sought all our lives.

After only a brief discussion about it (there wasn't any disagreement) we decided that we needed to learn how to do this properly and offer it to others, so that the gains would be permanent and safer for the seeker. We began our research on just what it was we were working with and investigated a variety of methods of emotion processing that all professed solutions, but each worked in significantly differing degrees of effectiveness.

After traveling lots of places to receive training in a variety of methods and trying them all on ourselves and everyone else that was brave enough to permit us to experiment on them, we finally began to narrow down the collection to only a few that were consistently effective and that had enough flexibility to work on a wide variety of conditions. The methods needed to be physically and mentally healing, while affording the spiritual progress that was the real objective.

Simultaneously we began to meditate. Neither of us had a long background in meditation, nor did we escape to a monastery to hide in seclusion and practice the craft. We incorporated both meditation and emotion processing (applying to each other) into our daily routine, making it as much a part of our daily life as eating or bathing. We encouraged each other for support of maintaining the practice and stuck to it.

Carol Elaine Crane died on December 19, 2011. Prior to her departure from her physical vehicle she not only attained the level of consciousness that she had previously experienced, but far surpassed it. She developed an intuitive ability to talk with her Higher Self and shared what she had learned with all who were willing and receptive. With a true and unwavering devotion, with love and compassion for all, she demonstrated the highest goals of humanity and attained unqualified unity consciousness.

It has been with her continued guidance, since her departure from her physical vehicle, that any and all gains that I may have made have been made. It is in the spirit of Carol's love and compassion for the suffering of humanity that we humbly offer the contents of this book. This book offers only the tools to attain enlightenment, which is synonymous with healing. It is still incumbent upon you, the reader, to employ these tools in a dedicated practice of fearless self discovery and warrior like dedication.

If you do, you will find what all who have undertaken the task of raising their consciousness have found. You will find joy, happiness, and all the indescribable things that are what we all truly seek... all powered by love.

Chapter One:

Evolution

Whether you are aware of it or not, you are on an evolutionary journey. You have already experienced many parts of this excursion and have many more to go before you will have finished the journey. If you are reading this, you are currently in the phase of the process that permits you experience the journey as a human on earth.

Contrary to popular opinion evolution has little or nothing to do with biological or physical adaptations and changes, other than how these adaptations and changes may affect your ability to have experiences. It has everything to do with the experiences that we have in life and how those experiences advance or regress consciousness for us individually and collectively as a population. In other words, evolution is about consciousness and in our case human consciousness because we are experiencing evolution right now as humans.

Throughout this writing we will make several statements, presented as fact that you may find contrary to your existing belief system or perspectives. We do not intend to offer long justifications for these statements. We do not ask that you accept these as presented, but rather we strongly suggest that you question them. Question everything! In the next chapter we will show you how to talk with your Higher Self (read; "listen" to your Higher Self). We invite you to discuss anything and everything with your Higher Self that we include in this writing and use this (Higher Self) as your independent source for substantiation. Any and all verification and substantiation is available directly from your Higher Self.

Enlightenment is a measurable way point on the evolutionary journey. Relative to other steps that we may have experienced up to this point, it is a very significant step because it is a point of progress offering a significant increase in awareness of who we are and who we are not. It is a point where taking control of our evolutionary path permits us to choose which path of the journey we will follow and how quickly we will continue. It is a dramatic point of development/attainment of consciousness when compared to where we currently are, or have been.

In order to have a grasp of enlightenment as a state of being that is real and attainable it is helpful to have a basic understanding of consciousness and what it is. In order to do this it may be necessary to surrender many popular or conventional understandings and consider consciousness from a universal/infinite perspective. It is very difficult to understand what is outside of the box by viewing it only from within the box.

All of creation was begun by the One Infinite Creator so that the Creator might "know itself". All is One. Everything is the Creator.

In order to facilitate creation, the Creator installed or created within itself a distortion. This distortion was/is the concept of Freewill. This distortion (Freewill) has permitted the creation and operation of all of what we perceive of as creation by promoting the perception that we are separate from the Creator.

As a result of this Distortion that we call Freewill the Creator's undistorted consciousness (entomological limitations are in play here) remains in tact, which is called "Intelligent Infinity", and the aspect of the Creator which has been distorted is called simply "Consciousness". Consciousness as we experience it is Intelligent Infinity, distorted by Freewill so that we may create and experience Creation from the perception that we are separate from the Creator. Consciousness, as we experience it, becomes a variable tool which can be used to create infinite opportunities for the Creator to experience itself.

One of the most profound elements of our experience of creation is that of evolution. Figuratively speaking, because no actual motion occurs, the process of evolution sends Consciousness "away" from the Creator by reducing the quantity/level of consciousness into creation and constructing a scenario where that casting away of consciousness is reeled back to the Creator through the occurrence of experience and the magnetic attraction of Source Energy (the Creator). Cast outward Consciousness strives to amalgamate and consolidate itself into a more unified Consciousness to eventually reunite with the Creator at the end of evolutionary cycle. This consolidation of "cast away" consciousness is represented by each individual person/being, unique in all of creation because each individual personality has been formed by the uniqueness of our experiences on the journey, all because of freewill.

Along the way, the "reeling in" of the "cast out" consciousness affords the opportunity to establish stratified ranges of consciousness. As consciousness is first cast away we enter the first defined range named First Density, with all Densities being so distinguished by the ratio of "Spiritual Mass" (AKA Consciousness) and "Intelligent Energy". The greater the Spiritual Mass the more spiritually advanced (AKA more aligned with the Creator) the Density. Conversely, the greater the ratio of Intelligent Energy and the lower the ratio of consciousness the less spiritually advanced the level and the lower the Density.

Intelligent Energy is what we know as the physical world (AKA Light). All that we perceive through our senses as the "real" physical world is Intelligent Energy/Light. For the sake of easy understanding, inorganic matter would be near to the extreme of "cast away" consciousness in First Density and comprises the physicality of creation.

After learning the experiences of First Density and amalgamating sufficient Consciousness to move into the range of Second Density, we become organic which preserves the physicality of First Density and blends it with the higher Consciousness of Second Density. We accumulate experiences by living as plants and animals, "conscious" but not self aware. We continue to gather Consciousness by learning from experiences in Second Density until we have amassed enough Spiritual Mass to move into Third Density, the Density we currently enjoy at this time.

Each Density consists of a range of consciousness that we move through by having experiences, learning the lessons of that Density, and "qualifying" for the next Density by virtue of our ability to "do the work" of the next level. These ranges have a bottom and a top, creating the limits of that Density. The range also can be measured in percentages, the bottom being zero percent and the top being 100% of capacity of that range.

Dr. David Hawkins, in his insightful book "Power v Force", creates a Scale of Human Consciousness to delineate even more definitively the range of consciousness. (Please note that this scale and the 0 to 100% scale are designed to measure only the human range of consciousness in Third Density. The total range of Consciousness in Creation is infinite.) Dr. Hawkins converts the percentage range to a scale ranging from 1 to 1000 and correlating levels of progress of Consciousness accumulation with human behavior and emotions. All people worldwide who have amalgamated Consciousness to a certain level on the Human Consciousness Scale will demonstrate similar behavior, with cultural difference being the only differentiating characteristic. No matter what the level of Consciousness, people with a corresponding level of Consciousness will demonstrate the same basic behavior and have equivalent capacity for experience. People reaching the benchmark of Enlightenment will, with few exceptions, essentially have the same types of experiences and demonstrate very similar behavior.

While in our current Density we are to learn the lessons of Love and Compassion sufficiently to graduate to the next Density. Because this is the first level of Consciousness that is self aware there are significant landmark occurrences as we move through our Density. Included among these landmark occurrences are attainment of the level of experiences of integrity, "Universal Love", and "Enlightenment". Being able to really "feel" love (not to be confused with the co-dependant attachment to another person promulgated in media, love stories, and advertising) occurs at the level of about 500 (50%). Universal Love, the feeling of love for all humanity, occurs about 540 (54%). The true experience of tranquility/peace (the underlying objective of desire) occurs at about 600 (60%). Enlightenment occurs about 700 (70%).

Please make a special note that we emphasis the importance of "feeling"! Evolution is not an intellectual or academic process. The more you strive towards Enlightenment through an intellectual understanding, the more you are resisting the process. We are pandering to the distortion of human intellectual needs by offering the information in this chapter, because very little of it is going to advance you along the Consciousness scale to any degree as we will illustrate in coming chapters.

Enlightenment is not the end of the journey within our level of Consciousness. After a person attains the level of Enlightenment there is still another 300 (30%) to go. Considering that major portions of the world population remain below 200 (20%), 300 points on the Human Scale of Consciousness is a lot of experiencing to experience. Also, as you near the 1,000 mark the climb to the top gets more and more difficult. The top of the mountain is always more steep than the bottom. Enlightenment may be described as a learner's permit meaning we finally have enough Consciousness to seriously begin to learn to drive in traffic to hone our abilities.

 The process of evolution begins with an absolute clean slate. We are the Creator. We have no emotional baggage that would cause us to know anything but the bliss of the Creator. However, because of freewill we begin to perceive ourselves separate from the Creator and with this perception we begin to have experiences. We have these experiences by experiencing them (AKA choosing them) with the application of emotion. Feelings! We feel things, not "think" about things. The Creator can "think" about things without us, but to truly know something, it must be felt.

You may read every book written about a flower and become the world's greatest authority on that flower, but until you actually experience that flower you cannot "know" that flower. You must touch its leaves and petals. You must smell it's scent. You must see the vibrant colors and its radiance.

The same is true of our life experiences and the purpose for evolution and creation itself. We must see, hear, taste, smell, and touch life. However, with Third Density consciousness we must do more. We must feel the emotions of life and then begin to employ wisdom by using our "intellect" to develop discernment, (AKA "put the intuitive input into useable order"). In so doing we begin to know life and fully experience life in this Density of consciousness.

As we experience life in these ways we begin to collect emotional baggage within our energy system. As we experience life the Creator also shares our experience of life, since we are an indivisible part of the Creator, and expands its knowingness of itself. As you collect this emotional baggage (forming biases and prejudices) you obscure and burden your vital energy, causing you to further perceive yourself as being even more separated from the Creator.

This emotional baggage is not a bad thing; it is just how evolution works. Emotional baggage is what makes you unique and permits the Creator to experience every occurrence within Creation uniquely. However, this emotional baggage is also the source of all suffering and all pain in our level of Consciousness (Third Density). Pain and suffering becomes the catalyst to move us forward on the evolutionary path.

This is the evolutionary journey. This is the Tao, Dharma, the Way, or whatever philosophical interpretation you choose to identify it with. We begin to learn the foundations for experiences in First Density. We continue the path in Second Density by learning the foundations of emotions and we accelerate the evolutionary process in Third Density by having more complex emotions, experiences, and beginning to employ wisdom, all the while piling heaps of emotional baggage upon our energy system to carry with us.

If you haven't noticed yet, the entire evolutionary process is conducted with and as energy. We are energy beings. Totally! There is no part of us that is composed of matter, even though we perceive it is such. We, and everything that we perceive, are created by applying consciousness to Intelligent Energy. Everything! Regardless of how many billions of dollars science spends on the search for "the God Particle" it will never be found because it doesn't exist.

With few exceptions, each of us begins the evolutionary process with the same quantity of Consciousness. It is entirely the Creator's energy, so it is all exactly the same... perfect and undifferentiated. However, because we begin interpreting experiences with the perception of freewill, we begin to distort this perfection and begin to differentiate ourselves by storing the energy/emotions within our own little private energy/emotion storage vault creating our personality and uniqueness.

As these energy/emotions accumulate they become more of a burden to us by requiring more of our vital energy to carry them and inhibit the free flow of the Creator's energy from flowing through us. Eckhart Tolle has named this accumulation of energy/emotions "the Pain Body", which well defines the condition. Our pain and suffering magnify. As this energy, in the form of emotions, accumulates we perceive ourselves as being further and further separated from the Creator. We are attempting to "turn our own wheel of fate" as we experience more and more pain and suffering, lifetime after lifetime, until we awaken.

Many people have heard of "Awakening", or even professed to have awakened, without really knowing what awakening is. Awakening is nothing more than realizing that you are actually in charge, or need to be in charge of your life. You begin to understand the process and take control of your life experiences. To do this, in and of itself, is consciousness raising but incomplete.

Having awakened what to do? You have realized something needs to be changed, and you desire to feel better, but how to do that?

Let's review for just a minute. Evolution is a process. It is not a competition to see who can get to the finish line (reunification with the Creator) first. The purpose of evolution, and creation itself, is to provide the Creator with opportunities to have experiences so that it might know itself.

You are an indivisible part of the Creator, within the evolutionary process, and designed to fulfill the Creator's desire to know itself. You are the only one that felt and stored the emotions from your lifetimes of experience, and you are the only one that knows how they have been stored, zipped up, tied in, and made you the living uniqueness that you are. Expecting someone else to do this for you is like sending a three year old to your bedroom, with the lights off, to find your favorite piece of jewelry that you have hidden to keep it safe.

No one can unzip or untie your load of emotional baggage except for you. You were the only one that felt them when you put them there, and you are the only one that can release them. Releasing them is essential in cleaning your energy (AKA "healing") to be able to move along the evolutionary path. You and your "Higher Self" (there is a reason your Higher Self is your Higher Self and not referenced as a vague Higher Power or Guide) must do the work and you are the part of this team that is "in the swamp". Your Higher Self can give you lots of help, but you must actually implement the guidance.

The end of the Third Density is the graduation to the next Density. The end of the evolutionary process is ultimately the reunification with the Creator. Raising your consciousness and working towards these conclusions is why you are here. It is an individual process and there are no group deals or short cuts.

Chapter Two

Talking to your Higher Self

The work that you perform to progress towards Enlightenment is best performed with the guidance of a master who knows the steps necessary to accomplish this task, and hopefully one that knows you so well that they can guide your every step without faltering. The being that can best meet that job requirement is your Higher Self. Your Higher Self has been your guide, not just for this lifetime, but throughout your entire evolutionary journey, and will remain so for the balance of your journey. If you have not already met your Higher Self and begun an earnest communication with them, it is time to do so.

Your Higher Self is your best friend in all of creation. Your Higher Self knows everything that there is to know about you. They know every thought that you have ever had. They know everything that you have ever done (or not done). They have your best interest at heart and love you completely, sincerely, and unconditionally.

It is a great honor/duty to guide a soul through the evolutionary process and each and every Higher Self accepts this honor/duty with the same degree of commitment and sense of responsibility. If ever you were going to establish an intimate and candid communication with another being, this is the one you want to establish it with.

Your Higher Self is "you" in the future. As explained in Chapter One, you/we are currently enjoying the evolutionary process in Third Density. Your Higher Self is currently in Sixth Density. For perspective purposes that is the consciousness difference between you/us and the level of consciousness one step below rocks (if there was one). They are outside of time and their interaction with your life is non-linear.

Your Higher Self has a personality which it developed as it progressed through its own evolutionary adventure and further honed as it worked itself through your evolution and those of your brothers and sisters that share your Higher Self, and there are many. Your Higher Self has a gender and a body, but a light body only. It is highly probable that they also have a sense of humor very similar to yours, or at least can appreciate yours. If you think about it, they must, because they put up with you all these lifetimes.

Your Higher Self will never trick you, never lie to you, and never do anything that may shake your confidence in them. They really don't care if you win the lottery or become president of Uruguay, unless winning the lottery or becoming president of Uruguay will advance you along the evolutionary spiritual path by providing you with opportunities for experience that you need to learn from. That is their primary concern, to help you fulfill your plan that you made before your incarnation, and your master plan that was set forth before you began your journey many years and lifetimes ago, to advance and grow spiritually and eventually to reunite with the Creator.

Your Higher Self is your best teacher. Through your Higher Self you can learn anything you want to know, except what is going to happen in the future. If you want, for some reason, to know what Abraham Lincoln had for breakfast on April 23, 1853, you can know that. If you want to know if Jesus was born on December 25, you can know that. (He wasn't, by the way.) If you want to know if there really is a Higgs-Boson Particle or how time and gravity really and truly work, you can know that too. You can know anything that you want to know about the past or the present.

You cannot know the future because you haven't experienced it yet. You have not lived that portion of your life. You must first make the choices of life by selecting from the infinite range of possibilities how you are going to interpret every moment of your life. Your Higher Self will not disclose any information that will infringe upon your freewill choices or those of anyone else!

Your Higher Self will also not allow itself to be used for commercial purposes. You cannot use your Higher Self so that you can become a psychic and charge people for answers. If your intent (and your HS knows your intent) is to take your communication and write a book to gain power and control over others, you probably will not receive co-operation from your Higher Self. However, if you seek the same information, and it doesn't infringe upon your or anyone else's freewill, and the intent is to aid all of mankind, you can probably receive the information.

Your Higher Self has a plan for you, and it is a plan that you helped make before you incarnated on Earth. The plan includes important things like what you need to learn to advance your journey along the evolutionary path. It is a detailed plan including every significant aspect of your life, but it is also a flexible plan. The plan can, and often does, change as you make life decisions.

You can know this plan, including your purpose in life. You can choose to follow the plan, or not follow the plan. As with most people before they learn to talk to their Higher Self, I suspect you have not been following the plan most of your life, but rather have been "turning your own wheel of fate". Wouldn't it be easier to just ask your Higher Self what the plan is and simply follow the plan that you and your Higher Self made for you?

The ability to both talk to and hear your Higher Self is something that we can all do. It does not require any predisposition towards psychic ability or intuitiveness. It will require some work on your part to develop your concentration and awareness. That is where meditation plays a part. (More on this in a later chapter.)

What we are going to teach you is to be used like a training wheel. It is not intended to be the end result. Only your commitment to develop your concentration and awareness and daily practice will improve your communication with your Higher Self. You may continue to use the training wheel and maintain a limited communication, or you may exert the effort to further expand upon your abilities. It's your choice, but the opportunity is there for you to develop.

Your Higher Self already communicates with you through dreams (direct communication from your Higher Self), through animals, through songs on the radio, telepathically, and through countless other little messages throughout your life. The only problem is your unawareness of these efforts to communicate with you. You can change that now.

If you do not already have a dream interpretation book and an animal spirit guide book, go get one of each. It doesn't matter if it is a good one or the "right" one, your Higher Self will know what resources you have and use those to communicate with you. (Don't get an animal spirit guide book that only has Amazon jungle animals in it if you live in Kansas. You probably won't see many black panthers or anacondas in your backyard.)

Keep a note pad and pen by your night stand (along with your dream interpretation book) to record your dream as soon as you awaken. Before going to bed, write the question you would like answered on the note pad. If you have difficulty remembering your dreams, before you get out of bed in the morning, depress your right nostril and breathe only through your left nostril for two to three minutes, then revisit your dream and see if your recollection isn't better.

After you record your dream, ask your Higher Self if the dream is from them. If it is (and it almost always will be), ask your Higher Self to confirm your interpretation step by step. "Did you mean this? Or, did you mean that?" Ask if the dream is prophetic or instructional. Ask if it is about you personally, or to be used with you as representative of a larger perspective. Compare it to your question and see if it doesn't provide an answer for you. The answers will be usually general, but may also have some specific aspects to it and will probably deal with the spiritual principals of your inquiry.

Become aware of animals that you see throughout the day. If you see a robin land close to you and it catches your eye, or a hawk floating lazily overhead, ask your Higher Self "is that a messenger from you?", if it is then go look up what the book says about that animal. When reading through the description of what accompanies that animal, inquire of your Higher Self which line of the description about the animal is the heart of their message.

You can use a tarot deck of cards with good descriptions of each card. Ask your Higher Self a question, such as "please show me what I can expect from the week?" Shuffle the deck and draw a card. Ask your Higher Self if the card is from them. If it is, see if it doesn't apply to the question. Reinsert the card in the deck; ask your High Self "if that card was really from you would you please show it to me again?" When you draw a card, see if it isn't the same card.

Ask your Higher Self if you could have a song that they could use to send you a pat on the back. Choose a song (any song, current or past but past is better, that is likely to be played on a radio station you listen to often). If you listen only to Country and Western music, it's not likely that you will hear Mozart's Toccata and Fugue in D Minor any time soon even with your Higher Self's efforts. If they agree, when you hear the song, ask your Higher Self if it was from them. They won't all be, but you will often hear it soon after you do something to help others or that advances your spiritual journey.

Talking to your Higher Self:

As you may have discerned from our presentation in the first part of this chapter your Higher Self is very interactive with your life. A successful communication with your Higher Self requires a degree of awareness on your part and a willingness to provide a mechanism that your Higher Self may use to communicate. Communication will eventually develop so that you simply sit down and have a casual conversation with your Higher Self, or, by finding stillness within you, taking control of your mind, and learning to discern your Higher Self's telepathic communication from your own thoughts you may experience an intense learning session with the use of these methods.

That is our eventual intent, for you to develop your talents so that you may communicate with your Higher Self with complete confidence and at will. In the mean time, this training wheel method we offer now can provide you with the tools necessary to begin to work towards this end. Your Higher Self is "at the ready" to assist you with this with only your asking and effort to do so. Never be hesitant to ask them for help. They are waiting in the wings for your invitation.

To begin, you will need to obtain a weight ranging from between 5 pounds and 15 pounds (more or less dependant upon your physical strength). Based upon our experience, most females will find a weight somewhere between 5 and 10 pounds most suitable and most men will find between 8 and 15 pounds most adequate. A dumbbell will do nicely, or for many people a one gallon jug of water will do since the full jug (of water) will weight 8 pounds. The water level may be adjusted to obtain the proper weight. We will be asking our Higher Self if the weight you are using is the proper weight, so for now, we are trying to get to that point.

Place the weight on a flat surface so that it will be on a relative par with your shoulder. If you are seated in a chair a table will do nicely. If you are seated on the floor a coffee table or end table may do. If you are standing you will need to have a ledge (fireplace mantle) or tall piece of furniture.

Your Higher Self is found in stillness. Close your eyes and find stillness within you. Take several deep breaths to do this if necessary. Take control of your mind by calming your thoughts as if you were preparing for meditation. Thinking of a loved one or just a happy memory will often be helpful.

With the weight on the flat surface and your shoulder on a relative par with the weight, extend your arm (either arm will do) fully so that your elbow does not bend (this is important). Grasp the weight and lift it a few inches straight up. The proper weight should be heavy to lift, but not so heavy that you strain your back muscles to lift it. This is not to be a demonstration of physical strength.

If the weight seems to qualify and while it is on the flat surface, make a statement that you know to be true, for example: "My name is (insert your name)." Pause for a second or two after finishing the statement and lift the weight again making a mental note of how heavy the weight felt. Return the weight to the table.

Make another statement that is the inverse of the first statement, for example: "My name is (make up a name)." Wait a few seconds and lift again, again making a mental note of how heavy the weight felt. Return the weight to the table. There should be a distinct difference between the two lifts. The true statement will prompt a distinctly lighter lift than the false statement.

Make another statement: "My Higher Self is with me" and lift, making mental note of the feel of the weight. Then repeat the exercise stating the inverse: "My Higher Self is not with me." The same phenomena, of the negative statement being distinctly heavier than the positive statement, should have occurred.

Note; always ask the inverse of your question to insure you are getting good communication and not getting false positive responses. A false positive response is one where either both lifts are strong/light, or both lifts are weaker/heavy.

Congratulations. You are communicating with your Higher Self.

If the difference between the two lifts is not distinctly different, try a heavier weight until you can clearly distinguish a difference between the two lifts.

If you are still not able to distinguish between the two lifts after increasing the weight until it is too heavy for you to lift, you will need to balance your energy to try again. Locate your Thymus gland underneath the top portion of your breast plate, about three inches straight down from the U-shaped dip at the base of your throat. Thump this location with your fist about six times. (Hard enough to make a thumping sound but not so hard as to hurt yourself.)

This will temporarily reset your body's meridian energy flow so that you will be able to work. You may need to do this periodically throughout a work period if you suddenly begin to get false positive answers or become unable to distinguish between the two lifts.

If you are working and loose your ability to distinguish between the two lifts, and the thumping method doesn't re-establish your ability to do so, you will need to walk away and leave it for 30 minutes to an hour. Do something to change your mood (for the better) or just relax. Also, you should not be under the influence of any drugs or alcohol, or hung over. You will not get good answers. Excessive fatigue or a prolonged illness may also distort the responses.

If you are unable to consistently get "good" and clear answers it is probable that your energy system is very jumbled and/or under significant duress. This will occur with people suffering from known or unknown trauma, addicts, or others simply experiencing high levels of stress. If this does not work for you and the correcting methods do not permit you to use the system you can still begin to heal and soon be able to use this system by going to Chapter Five and employing the "Trauma Release and Basic Healing Method".

Answers that require a number or name may be difficult to obtain. In your mind, picture a computer screen, piece of writing paper, blackboard, or any other type of writing display that is easy for you to visualize. One man who was learning this method could easily picture a billboard, which was fine. Ask your Higher Self to write the answer on the item you are visualizing and then watch/listen. Use the weight to confirm or deny what you thought you saw. If you get it wrong, politely ask them to do it again until you get a confirmation that what you saw/heard is correct.

You may have a raft of questions to pose already. If you don't, we have prepared several that you may want to practice with to learn how to pose your questions.

After you ask your question always pause and listen to hear what is being communicated to you. When you think you have the answer, use the weight to confirm or deny it. If you get it wrong, ask them to give it to you again. The weight will give you true/false, yes/no, answers all day long, but you want to learn to hear what your Higher Self is communicating to you telepathically, so learn to listen.

Sample Questions:

My name is (insert your name).

My name is (insert a wrong name).

My Higher Self is with me.

My Higher Self is not with me.

I am participating in an evolutionary process.

I am not participating in an evolutionary process.

I am currently incarnate in a Third Density experience taking place on Earth.

I am not currently incarnate in a Third Density experience taking place on Earth.

Enlightenment is a measurable way point on the evolutionary journey.

This is not the case.

Evolution is about the evolution of consciousness.

This is not the case.

All of creation was begun by the One Infinite Creator so that the Creator might "know itself".

This is not the case.

All is One.

All is not One.

Everything is the Creator.

This is not the case.

You (my Higher Self) can and will guide me in my quest to become Enlightened.

This is not the case.

The methods taught in this book will provide me with the tools to become enlightened.

This is not the case.

In order for me to become enlightened it will be necessary for me to diligently employ the tools taught to me in this book.

This is not the case.

It is in your plan for me to become enlightened.

This is not the case.

It is in your plan for me to experience joy greater than I have known during my current incarnation.

This is not the case.

I cannot know the future if it may infringe upon my freewill or the freewill of others.

I can know the future whether it will infringe upon my freewill or other freewill or not.

You have been attempting to communicate with me my whole life.

This is not the case.

It is in your plan for me to develop a close relationship with you and have clear communication.

This is not the case.

If I choose a song that may be played on the radio you will periodically send me the song as a confirmation that you are with me.

This is not the case.

It will be satisfactory with you to use (insert the name of the song and artist) to facilitate this communication.

This song will not be satisfactory.

To begin to employ the healing methods and incorporate your communication with your Higher Self investigate the following:

It is my Higher Self's recommendation that I learn and employ the Trauma Release and Basic Healing method (Chapter Five) as described in this book as my first method.

It is not my Higher Self's recommendation that I learn and employ the Trauma Release and Basic Healing method (Chapter Five) as described in this book as my first method.

It is my Higher Self's recommendation that I learn and employ the Moving Emotions/Energy method (Chapter Seven) as described in this book as my first method.

It is not my Higher Self's recommendation that I learn and employ the Moving Emotions/Energy method (Chapter Seven) as described in this book as my first method.

It is my Higher Self's recommendation that I learn and employ the Dissolving Emotions/Energy method (Chapter Eight) as described in this book as my first method.

It is not my Higher Self's recommendation that I learn and employ the Dissolving Emotions/Energy method (Chapter Eight) as described in this book as my first method.

It is my Higher Self's recommendation that I learn and employ the Integrating Polarities of Emotions/Energy method (Chapter Nine) as described in this book as my first method.

It is not my Higher Self's recommendation that I learn and employ the Integrating Polarities of Emotions/Energy method (Chapter Nine) as described in this book as my first method.

It is my Higher Self's recommendation that I learn and employ the Bodhisattva Enlightenment method (Chapter Ten) as described in this book as my first method.

It is not my Higher Self's recommendation that I learn and employ the Bodhisattva Enlightenment method (Chapter Ten) as described in this book as my first method.

Ask your higher Self to "energize" your heart (Heart Chakra) and then just feel for your heart to be energized (vibrate). It is appropriate to offer gratitude for your Higher Self's love and support for you. After doing so, listen for their response.

Chapter Three

Emotional Baggage

Understanding of evolution, the journey to Enlightenment, is greatly aided with the understanding that all of Creation exists so that the Creator may know itself. (Since you now know how to ask your Higher Self questions you may confirm or deny this and everything else we present to you.) The creation of consciousness by the injection of freewill into a portion of Intelligent Infinity (as explained in Chapter One) provided the Creator with the vehicle to accomplish this. This also was the creation of the first polarity with one portion being that of the Creator that perceives itself separate from the Creator (Consciousness) and the undistorted Intelligent Infinity portion of the Creator.

Polarity is important in our experience because it is the basic perceptual construct of our experience. Other equally productive constructs exist within creation, but we are in one of the structures that function with a dualistic operating system. We perceive things as high/low, hot/cold, good/bad, male/female, etc. These are only perceptions on our part, because in truth it (we) is all one, as is the perception that we are separate from the Creator.

What actually exists is entropy. Simply explained, entropy is a scale. Science will explain entropy as a scale of energy, or heat, whereby one end of the scale is absolutely hot and the other absolutely cold, or absolutely anything on one end and the opposite extreme on the other end. This defines the evolutionary process as well. On the top of the evolutionary scale is absolute stability, the Creator. On the other end of the scale is absolute chaos (the cast away portion of the Creator). Between the two extremes is creation and we exist somewhere in between.

Evolution is the process of casting away into lower consciousness portions of ourselves as the experiencial Creator. When I reference the separated or "cast away" portion of the Creator I am in no way suggesting that it is a cast out, or thrown away portion, but rather like a fisherman casting his fishing line and lure into the lake. The lure is still attached to the line and held firmly by the fisherman, but just projected away from the fisherman so that it may do its job. The fisherman still feels the line and controls the lure, but the lure has the freedom, within limits, to snare fish, its purpose. It's doing the job for which it was designed just as we are doing the job for which we were designed.

We begin evolution as the Creator, in absolute stability. We then are cast away from that stability, still a part of the Creator, to experience near absolute chaos. It is our task, in service to and as an undivided part of the Creator, to return to where we started from, an un-separated portion of the Creator and absolute stability. That is a basic characteristic of entropy that the system seeks stability.

We experience life and consequently follow the evolutionary path by having experiences. We have experiences through the feeling of emotions. Without feeling emotions we could not have experiences. It is by application of our emotions to any given experience that we choose what experiences we will have from an infinite range of possibilities.

The Creator comes to know itself through our emotions, not from what we think. So, as we experience life, the Creator experiences life. As we evolve (return to the Creator) the Creator accomplishes its goal of knowing itself. It's not a matter of us collecting all of these experiences and reporting to the Creator when we get home, the Creator gains benefit of our experiences immediately. Returning to the Creator is the process of completing the entire cycle of evolution.

As we are initially cast away from the Creator, we have very little consciousness and lots of Intelligent Energy to work with. Intelligent Energy (AKA Light) is the clay of creation form which everything is made. Consciousness applied to Intelligent Energy gives Intelligent Energy stability. Currently we are full of chaos, with not much stability because of our low consciousness. As we have experiences we begin to collect and consolidate consciousness and reduce our chaos. As we continue to do this up to the level of consciousness approximately where we are now, we also collect and store emotions within our energy system (AKA Chakras). Once we have gathered enough consciousness to do so, we awaken and gain awareness of how the process of evolution works, but we have also amassed a large quantity of emotions within our energy system.

The accumulation of stored emotional energy that we carry within our Chakras begins to build a significant energy mass. Eckhart Tolle describes this mass as our "Pain Body" which is a very accurate description because we perceive the stored emotions to be within and part of our physical body. We feel them physically every time we experience fear and get a tightening in our stomach or a lump in our throat when we think about the loss of a loved one. Separation, the perceived separation from the Creator, is painful in and of itself and the mental anguish we create as a result of this causes suffering.

However, what we store is not all emotions from pain and suffering. Emotions from extremely positive experiences can be as inhibiting as the negative ones because they are not in balance. Balance is the key. The Buddha identified this condition of balance as equanimity. Awakening is the point whereby we knowingly take control of the process of evolution and decide not only to stop creating the pain and suffering, but to get rid of the emotional storehouse we have accumulated and start healing (AKA knowingly moving towards the Creator). We begin to direct our movement through the entropy heading ever more quickly towards stability.

Because the stored emotions do have the characteristics of mass they serve as blockages/hindrances to the free uninhibited flow of our vital energy. They require the diversion of our vital energy to hold themselves in place and as a direct result divert the energy necessary to live life in a productive manner and that permits us to consolidate more consciousness. A productive manner is one that permits us to learn and grow from our experiences in such a way as to be able to continue to merge consciousness and move us along the evolutionary path. We become/remain preoccupied with protecting ourselves from our emotions, surviving, collecting (AKA greed), and miss the whole purpose of our existence. We remain in low consciousness and behave accordingly with self perpetuating and ever expanding ignorance and a continuation of perceived separation from the Creator.

If you consider that this load of emotional baggage is like a 300 pound ball of concrete that we are carrying, it becomes obvious that it will be difficult to accomplish any of the things we had planned on or need to be doing with our life when we have to use all our energy just to carry the ball of concrete. Imagine if your goal is to run down to the end of the street. "No problem" you say as you put on your running shoes. But after you are dressed and ready to go you are told, "And, by the way, you have to carry this 300 pound of concrete on your shoulders." The task becomes almost impossible.

Of course the reality of the situation is that getting rid of the 300 pound ball of concrete is one of the primary objectives of our lifetime at this level of consciousness. It has become part of our experience. This emotional baggage is our ego (AKA "false self") and we will most often defend it to the death. It's not comfortable and it causes us continuous pain and suffering, but its familiar and its mine, so we are reluctant to get rid of it. While we remain asleep and in ignorance about our true nature we think it is all that we have, so we defend it. It causes us physical illness, mental illness, and keeps us in slavery, but we profess "by God I'm keeping it." Our ego is what is keeping us in the perception that we are separate from the Creator and dissolving our ego is what we will be working on for the next several Densities of our evolutionary journey. To reunite with the Creator at the end of the journey we must be as slick and clean as we were when we started.

If you are not ready to start taking chunks out of your 300 pound ball of concrete, that is perfectly OK. As we said before, evolution is not a race or a competition of any kind. It is an opportunity for the Creator to know itself and even those who choose to remain asleep are fulfilling that purpose. We can empathize with our brothers and sisters that choose to remain asleep and offer love and compassion for their condition, but our journey is an individual journey and we can choose to move forward on our own without regret.

Pain and suffering are our learning tools and our motivators. They bring our attention and focus to a condition within us that needs our attention. They accomplish this through messengers. The messengers are every person that we meet in our lives, whether they are with us for five minutes or fifty years. Every person in our lives is there for a purpose. They are bringing us a message and the message is never about them, it is always about us. If we feel an emotion, we need to learn to pay attention to it because that is our warning signal that there is something within us that needs to be released. Our awareness is being activated that there is emotional baggage that includes some aspect of the message that we are supposed to become aware of and get rid of.

We have all developed mechanisms for avoiding these messages, ranging from killing the messenger to pretending the message didn't come at all. Some of our mechanisms actually added additional emotional baggage all by themselves. Most of us will continue to collect emotional baggage and feel the pain and suffering until "the pain of staying the same is greater than the pain of change." When we reach that point, we will begin to change. We may be living on the street and dumpster diving for food, but that is our choice.

Learning to have gratitude for the difficulties that we experience in life is one of the things that will happen when we awaken and begin to take control of our lives by lessening our load and raising our consciousness. Through awareness of the emotions we are currently feeling we begin to recognize them as the friends that they are. Without the energy that they stimulate within us we would forever go through our days in ignorance and continue to repeat the same experiences over and over.

Everyone has had the experience of perpetually having to deal with the same person over and over. You may know as a "type", or as the one that always hurts you or disappoints you? It is not the person that is the same but the emotions and behavior that they trigger within you. The location is different, the experience is different, the time is different, and the person bringing you the message is different, but it's the same message in a different suit of clothing. What is the same? You! You feel the same emotions and identify the person as the same "type" of person, but it's really you that is the same. You are carrying the same emotional baggage from experience to experience; unable or unwilling to look inside to see the pain and suffering you are creating for yourself.

How you change this pattern is actually very simple but terribly frightening for a lot of people. You get rid of the emotional baggage that you are carrying. As you do, you gain stability. You allow your self to be reeled back in a little more, moving ever closer to the Creator and consolidating consciousness as you go.

Unloading the emotional baggage, like any worthwhile endeavor, will require an investment on your part. It will require diligence and commitment and a fearless delving into the inner you. The yardstick to how you are doing is happiness. The happier you are becoming the more progress you are making. The more you are able to love yourself and others, the greater your success until one day you awaken and realize "I feel good, and I'm happier than I have ever been."

As you work to unload the emotional baggage numerous things will happen to you. (Remember that you are actually working to raise your consciousness.) You will physically feel better (because physical health is a byproduct) and be mentally more alert. Mindfulness, the awareness of what is going on inside and outside, will improve. Such things as fears, phobias, and irritations with people will fade away. Such behaviors as over eating, addictions, stress, and hoarding will fade away and your whole lifestyle becomes more supportive of a higher consciousness. You begin to stop reacting to life and begin to be able to respond to life with the appropriate response.

From a social perspective bellicosity declines and eventually is eliminated. Crime declines and is eventually eliminated. Drug abuse, alcoholism, abusive medical systems, corporate greed, and all of our social ills repair themselves. Idealistic as all this may seem, remember that by raising our consciousness we are becoming aligned and moving toward reunion with the Creator. All of our personal and social ills are products of our perceived separation from the Creator.

As Dr. David Hawkins concludes in his research, behavior, both individual and societal, are a direct correlation of our level of consciousness. Raise both individual and collective consciousness and all behavior improves. This is also the repetitive teachings of "all" of our recognized spiritual teachers throughout recorded history.

Another task that we are to accomplish in this Density is to polarize. This polarization is demonstrated by how we live our lives, which includes not only how we act but also how we think. The choices are simple and the polarization is aptly characterized as choosing between "Service to Self" and

"Service to Others". If you decide to commit yourself to pursue Enlightenment you cannot help but polarize Service to Others. If you choose to polarize Service to Self you cannot attain Enlightenment but rather choose to remain in pain, suffering, and separated from the Creator.

Enlightenment facilitates increased energy creation, or more accurately, permitting the flow of Intelligent Infinity to flow through you. Service to Self polarization cannot create energy, and must steal energy/consciousness from others, which they are very adept at doing. This simple choice will determine your path through the balance of your evolutionary journey. The duality of our existence continues for many more years to come, but it is your choice as to how to experience it. Either path, Service to Self v Service to Others, is making a significant contribution to the Creator.

"The longest journey begins with a single step", the Chinese philosopher and Taoist Lao Tzu is quoted as saying, and this is very true. The journey began with you and must be carried on by you. You are on the journey already. Are you ready to get on with the fun part instead of remaining in the swamp and battling alligators?

Enlightenment, to be efficiently pursued, must be approached with a parallel complimentary process. On the one hand you must throw the emotional baggage off your cart, as we will teach you in this writing. You must begin to chip away at the 300 pound ball of concrete. While this may be difficult at first it will be the strength of your will that will garner sufficient energy to facilitate this. As you unload each piece of baggage you reclaim the energy you were using to hold that baggage in place and make it available to do more work. So, as you do the work, you have more energy to do even more work. You are initiating an upward spiral of energy that becomes self sustaining.

The other aspect of the enterprise is to learn to direct and control the energy that you have available and that is being added to by the unloading. This is done by meditation. If you only have the energy to follow one of these processes (just cannot meditate no matter how hard you try), then unload the baggage. Soon you will have the energy to either significantly improve or begin a productive meditation practice.

Chapter Four

Emotions

Evolution is an experiencial process and it is not necessary to be "smart" or well educated to evolve and reach Enlightenment. If it were only for smart people then only smart people need apply, but life is to be lived (and experienced) by everyone equally, without exception. Life is experienced by feelings which we identify as emotions. Anyone who feels emotions and can learn to develop concentration and awareness can attain Enlightenment.

Intellect and organization are the purview of the left hemisphere of the brain. It is the left hemisphere that accepts the intuition/information provided by the right hemisphere and puts it into useable order (AKA "Physicality"). As with all of life, it is balance between the two hemispheres that is sought rather than domination by either the right or left hemispheres.

As we have already explained, we have been learning to feel emotions for many lifetimes in this Density and previous Densities as well. In the process of learning to feel emotions we have been collecting emotional baggage (AKA creating the "Pain Body") which consists of low vibration energy stored within our energy body. It is literally stuck/sluggish energy/emotions. This emotional baggage comprises our 300 pound ball of concrete that we carry with us everywhere we go. It is the essence of our ego (AKA our separateness/false self) which is the pain body displaying its influence in the form of biases and prejudices and shaping our personality that we present to the world of other beings.

It is possible, but not probable, for us to simply release all of the emotional baggage that we have collected, dissolve the pain body, surrender all of our biases, prejudices, ego, and return home to total unity (AKA finish our evolutionary journey by reuniting with the Creator). However, the journey is designed to be a process and simply throwing all the emotional baggage off of the cart at once is not the design and does not fulfill the intent of evolution. The design is to incrementally throw off pieces of baggage that we have collected a piece at a time (of course it may be a steamer trunk), thereby providing additional experience as we proceed.

In this chapter we will give you an over view of Emotion Processing, identified in the previous chapter as one of two activities to be employed to experience Enlightenment. Emotion Processing is a spiritual technology. It heals unwanted physical, mental, and emotional issues by focusing on the root cause of illness and disease which we broadly identify as stored emotional energy. This stored emotional energy (emotional baggage) lowers our consciousness and restricts our progress along the evolutionary path.

Traditionally this emotional baggage has been taught to be resolved primarily through meditation. After developing sufficient concentration and awareness over many years and through a rigorous practice of calming the mind and learning to focus the mind inside ourselves we identify this emotional baggage and work to release it. Through meditation we strive to accomplish the same end results as emotion processing. The release is/was facilitated by intense awareness, "shinning the light of our consciousness" into the darkness that we had stored. This method is still very effective, but very slow and tedious by comparison to emotion processing methods.

Beginning in the 1950's a new form of spiritual technology was discovered which expedites the process of achieving the same results that traditional meditation had been doing for thousands of years. Emotion Processing has progressed incrementally as our understanding of its true nature revealed itself, allowing us just recently to recognize its full potential. Today, these methods have matured to a significant degree and can now, with the methods offered in this writing, be best self applied by each and every individual with the guidance and assistance of the Higher Self. That is our intent with this book, to provide each and every individual with the tools to relieve the emotional baggage and mental constructs (biases and prejudices) that hinders our attainment of increased human consciousness and physical, emotional, and mental healing.

Some less effective methods have been recognized by therapist, psychologists, and psychiatrist and classified as "Energy Psychology". No matter who uses these techniques in whatever professional setting or classification, your best practitioner is you, and your best guide is your Higher Self. The reason that they have been recognized by these professions is that they provide healing dramatically more quickly and completely than any traditional or competing methodology ever devised, as you will soon experience. When you replace the human element, such as your therapist, guide, or processor, and substitute your Higher Self in this role you become a "healing machine" with no limit to gains you can make.

Each of us is unique in all of creation. However, what makes us unique is not what you may think. Vital energy, the essence of who we are, is exactly the same in each one of us, and in the same quantity without exception. This undistorted vital energy is what we started evolution with and what we will need to complete the evolutionary process. Some if it remains in potentiation only because we have not yet tapped the depth of our resources.

What makes us a unique individual is the distortion of this vital energy that we have created by virtue of our interpretation of experiences and the manner in which we have stored the emotional baggage that we collected during the evolutionary process. Some of us stored it sideways. Some of us stored it vertically. Some of us stored it in a herringbone pattern. Most of us stored it in a haphazard "throw it on the pile" fashion. All of the storing of this emotional baggage, no matter how it was stored, causes us to descend into chaos, away from the stability of the Creator.

Because we are the only ones that felt the emotions as we experienced them we are the only ones that know how we buttoned them up, laced them up, and zipped them up and we are the only ones that can get them out. There is a reason your Higher Self is called your Higher Self and not the Higher Power or Higher "Somebody Else". Your Higher Self is "You". It too knows how you stored this emotional baggage and can help/guide you to discover and release this energy. Your Higher Self is in the press box and can see the whole field, while you are on the field playing the game. They have a much better vantage point from which to direct your efforts.

Emotions, and how we experience them, are not difficult to understand. Emotions are our pointer that we use to choose our experiences. It is through the application of our emotions to any potential experience that we choose the experience that becomes our primary path for life. If we live our life with a predisposition towards fear, we will attract/choose fear based experiences. If you are predisposed towards anger, courage, shame, despairs, etc., those are the chosen emotions. Emotions are just a variety of vibrating ranges of energy, held in place by our own consciousness. We experience what we create with our choices.

We do not have experiences in the physical world. That may seem like a remarkable statement since we perceive that we can experience nothing but the physical world, but it's true. Experiences occur in the metaphysical world (AKA "Time/Space"). It is through the application of emotions that we choose the potential experience out of an infinite number of possibilities and bring it into our existence. No experience can move into space/time (our "real" world) without the application of emotion no matter how seemingly subtle. (Our limited level of consciousness causes us to perceive a seamless flow of cause and effect experiences, all within the perceived physical world.)

Within our current level of consciousness we have a range of potential emotional experience. The middle of this range is balance. At one end of the range is our most positive energy extreme and at the other end is our most negative energy extreme. This range of emotional energy is pretty much the same for everyone within our level of consciousness with the positive extreme being as distorting as the negative extreme because it is out of balance. The more heavily burdened we are with emotional baggage the more likely we will gravitate to the more extreme outer edges of the emotional range.

The instant of experience is put into motion as time. We apply an appropriate emotion to each instant within time ("time dot"), bringing it into our existence and creating a series of contiguous dots forming a "time line". The emotion that we apply to each time dot will be selected unconsciously as long as we remain asleep and perceive ourselves a victim of circumstance as we create a time line. When we awaken, we begin to be able to choose/apply the appropriate energy/emotion, rather than relying upon our biases and prejudices to select the emotion of the moment, therefore changing our whole experience of life.

Underneath the emotions are biases and prejudices. We automatically and unconsciously use biases and prejudices to direct the experience life. Underneath the biases and prejudices are what is called mental constructs. Unadjusted, these mental constructs keep us on path to remain unconscious and reinforce the biases and prejudices that have become habitual. The mental constructs may be where the real elements needing change reside but you must first release the multiple layers of emotional baggage. The emotional baggage cannot simply be skipped over or moved out of the way. They will continue to constitute a significant burden to your vital energy and will manifest one way or another until you release it completely from the energy system.

As long as our biases and prejudices, and the underlying mental constructs, remain our resource for emotion application and experience selection we remain in pain and suffering. Since our biases and prejudices are chaos (the far end of the stability scale from the Creator) and the underlying source of our pain body, we remain in low consciousness and asleep (unconscious). Our accumulated emotional baggage (pain body) therefore, keeps us in pain and suffering and away from the stability and bliss that alignment with the Creator provides.

Working towards Enlightenment is taking charge of the healing (evolution) enterprise. In order to be successful in the enterprise it is necessary to "do the work" (throw the emotional baggage off your cart". As you do this, you gain additional consciousness, additional stability, and eventually reach the foundational issues held within the self as mental constructs, permitting the experience of ever increasing happiness. Happiness/joy becomes the measure of how we are doing. The happier we are, the more progress we are making.

Beginning the awakening process and throwing the emotional baggage off of the cart is the most difficult part. It is much like pushing a stalled car. From a dead stop, it requires significant energy to get it moving but once you have it moving, momentum becomes a positive factor and makes it easier to push with less effort. Stopping the work requires you to again exert significant effort to re-start the work when momentum is lost. The wisdom here is "don't stop" once you start the healing process.

A common behavior is to stop the work when you feel better. Compared to how you used to feel you may mistakenly reach a point where you think you are done. However, it will probably only be a plateau and there is significantly more work to do. Discuss and review with your Higher Self the progress that you have made and how much more you have to do. Your Higher Self, we reiterate, is your guide, partner, and mentor. Allow them to measure your progress until you truly are finished.

In our writings, we have been hammering on emotions in such a way that it might be interpreted that emotions are bad thing and that we should avoid emotions and work to reach a state of "no emotion", but that is furthest from the truth. Without emotions we couldn't experience life. Our purpose is to feel life and learn to appreciate life through emotions. Without them we literally wouldn't be alive. We emphasis however, that we should not continue to carry our emotions after we have the experience. We must learn to let them lay where they were experienced. This becomes much easier once we unload the baggage we have already collected and stored.

In a single lifetime the process of collecting emotional baggage, forming biases and prejudices, and creating and/or reinforcing mental constructs begins at an early age. We begin and mostly complete our entire emotional foundation within the first seven years of our life (give or take a year or two).When we are a child, even at a precognitive age, we feel an unidentified energy (usually a negative energy). If the condition is quickly resolved we dismiss the feeling and go about being a baby/kid. However, when this negative energy is felt and not quickly resolved we form a thought and immediately begin to associate the thought with the negative energy. Once we have done this the first time we repeatedly, subconsciously, and automatically apply the same thought every time we feel that negative energy. We continue to do this as an adult until we become aware of our habitual behavior and remove the emotions associated with the "feel the negative energy" > "apply the thought" > "react" scenario.

For example: Assume you are an infant lying in your crib. You awaken in the middle of the night and feel the negative energy from hunger. The cause of the negative energy at this point is unimportant, only that you feel, at this point, an unlabeled negative energy. Mom or Dad has always been there Johnny on the Spot with a bottle to quell the hunger and the negative energy went away… no problem. This has been going on for six to eight weeks and Mom and Dad are worn out. They don't awaken immediately and you lie in your crib and cry for a bit longer than usual. No abuse or ill intent is in the making, Mom and Dad are just worn out.

Because you were allowed to feel this negative energy without relief within the expected period of time, you apply a thought to that feeling. The thought is always a simple thought such as "There is no one there for me", or "I'm all alone" or some other simple thought not rooted in rational or logic. It's never a long drawn out, or complete thought, just one sufficient to interpret or label the energy you are feeling. This then becomes a foundational emotion building experience for you. According to Dr. David Hawkins it only takes 1/10,000 of a second to hereafter subconsciously apply that thought to the negative feeling.

Another example: You are the youngest child and your older sibling and their friend repeatedly invade your space and play with your toys, excluding and even deriding you during these play sessions. No one intercedes to aid you in standing your ground. Since this happens repeatedly it may become a reoccurring source of a small trauma. Most would consider this as a common hazard of childhood, but each person stores energy and interprets life's experiences differently. Remember all such experiences are interpreted with a child's mind, not an adult rational mind. What may be easily dismissed as "no big deal" to an adult may be a life altering and hindering experience to a child.

An initial application of an erroneous thought to the negative energy felt, such as "I'm not good enough", "I'm not worthy", or "I don't deserve" and repeatedly reinforced by a sibling or role model would be consequential but not crippling as a child, but as the basis of adult behavior could be tremendously damaging. To the adult looking back upon the experience it may even seem silly or just part of childhood. However, once the trauma in established it subconsciously/energetically governs the person's ability to function in all aspects of their life.

As an adult, when you apply the thought to the negative energy that you feel, and you may feel it as a result of a myriad of adult catalyst, you prejudge the outcome of an experience before you even have the experience. Your decisions about a girlfriend or boyfriend's behavior are prejudged with the emotion stimulating thought that "there is no one there for me", creating a series of unfulfilling co-dependant relationships. Your decisions about survival security, job choices, spouse selection, and countless other smaller day to day decisions are all prejudged because you, deep down, really believe that "you are not good enough".

Is it true? No of course not. Is it rational or logical? No, certainly not. But regardless, it is a foundational emotion generating a condition that will lead you down a path of pain and suffering as long as you remain unconscious. Remember, we bring all experience into our "reality" with the application of emotion. If the emotion used is automatic, and selected prior to awareness of the experience we are compelled to use our biases and prejudices to live life. We remain asleep and continue to react to life, rather than be able to respond to life with wisdom. Our heavily burdened consciousness level (vital energy) doesn't have enough energy available to use wisdom to live life and more accurately gain a perspective of our experiences.

The total number of simple "thoughts" that people the world over apply to these foundational negative energy > thought situations is probably less than twenty-four, but the emotions range the full gamete. The first emotion that appears after you first apply the thought to the negative energy may be fear, or heart brokenness, or guilt. It doesn't matter what the label is, it has a negative energy vibration and that determines where within our energy system it will become lodged and will expose itself through a body sensation.

Fear, for example, is lodged/stored in our solar lexes and perineum. Guilt and shame are stored about two inches below our navel. Grief and heart brokenness are stored in our heart area. One or more of these then becomes our emotion of choice because of the vibration of the energy that we have associated with the thought habit. Each of these emotions is a vibrating range of energy and if the obstruction is allowed to remain will eventually manifest into physical illness or disease.

The universe is our teacher and gives us the tools and guidance to heal ourselves by awakening and becoming aware. In order to do this, it brings us new experiences that continue to trigger the emotions that we have stored. Time after time we encounter new opportunities for experience, always brought to us by people that will trigger the emotions that we have stored. People will repeatedly bring us experiences triggering fear, or, shame, or guilt to attempt to prompt us to look inside and see that the emotion is always within us. The emotional baggage becomes a magnet that says "kick me with fear, or guilt, or shame" so that I will awaken and look inside to heal myself.

The emotion(s) ("vibrating energy") that we have chosen is the energy string that links or ties all of our life experiences together. People who bring us the messages may be different, the places may be different, and each will occur at different times/stages of our life, but the one common thread is the emotion that we felt in each experience. This identification and recognition is the link to our life pattern. This is the message that we are to become aware of and the emotion/mental construct that we need to let go of.

People are always the messengers and teachers. Every person that comes into our life, whether for five minutes or a lifetime, is bringing us a message. The message is always about ourselves because we are the only ones that feel the emotion. Become aware of your life pattern and allow yourself to heal. This is how you learn to have love and compassion for yourself, which will lead to love and compassion for others, an important milestone on the path to Enlightenment.

Becoming aware requires a certain amount of energy/consciousness. Initially it may take all the energy you have just to start to do the work of Enlightenment. That's OK. Just do what you can. As you do the work you gain stability, strength, concentrative ability, and awareness. As you gain momentum and begin to release the emotional baggage and the energy that you were using to hold the emotional baggage in place, this energy is made available to you to do more work. The momentum of moving the ball begins to carry you forward at a faster and ever more efficient pace.

Chapter Five

Trauma Release and Basic Healing

Trauma is different from a simple emotion. Trauma results from a person being overwhelmed with a barrage of multiple emotions, or even one emotion that the body's subconscious protective systems deems to be too intense for the energy system to handle. Trauma significantly jumbles ones energy and leaves the person feeling less able to deal with life after the event than before.

Trauma may also result over a period of time from a series of smaller events that leave a person "shell shocked". The result is the same as a single event in that the person is left less able to deal with life after the series of occurrences has ceased than they were before the events began to happen. What constitutes a trauma for one person may not be the same for another person. This often times is a more difficult condition to identify because it incrementally adds another helping of the same energy/emotion to the pile of emotions already stored. The trauma response is always a self protective device that the body's energy system implements based solely upon the person's individual make up at the time that the experience(s) occurs.

Most of us experience trauma of one sort or another during our lifetime. Large numbers of us continue to carry this trauma and simply learn to accept it and the feeling of reduced vital energy as the new us. Traditional consensus is that we will learn to deal with it over time, or "get over it", but that is only adapting to the feeling of the new reduced level of vital energy. We are learning to live with less vital energy, but it isn't necessary to do this.

When we have a trauma we experience strong emotion(s). Anything that shakes our sensibilities or our sense of survival can create a trauma. In order to protect ourselves from the trauma energy/emotion we literally take part of our vital energy (spirit) to wrap around the bundle of strong emotions and lock them away inside our energy system so we won't have to deal with them. Wrapping the emotions within our vital energy is called a "trauma cap". When we create a trauma cap and allocate part of our vital energy to protect us from the emotions, we have less vital energy to deal with life. Our energy becomes jumbled and more chaotic.

Once we take a part of our vital energy to lock these emotions away we have less energy to deal with future strong experiences, so people that are carrying a trauma usually will have multiple traumas. This occurs because experiences that previously would have fallen well within the range of our ability to deal with them when we have 100% of our vital energy available to us now become traumas because we already used a portion of our vital energy to keep the first trauma emotions locked away thereby reducing our total available vital energy. For example, we may only have 80% of our vital energy to deal with an experience after the first trauma and we encounter a new experience that required 90% of our vital energy. As a result we must take additional vital energy to lock this new energy/emotion away to deal with what would have previously not been a trauma at all. We fall further and further behind the energy curve because with each subsequent trauma we must take additional vital energy to lock more and more emotions away. We sink further and further into chaos until our physical vehicle (body) no longer has enough energy to function.

In order to heal from a trauma(s) it is necessary to release the emotions associated with the trauma, but first we must release the trauma cap so that we can get to the emotions. A trauma cap doesn't usually respond to traditional treatments because it is a protective device for our energy body. Once the trauma cap is release we can fairly quickly dissipate the emotions on a one at a time basis, or if the person is not too heavily burdened with chaotic energy, work can be done on a more wholesale basis releasing whole blocks of related emotions/energy at one time.

A process called a "Trauma Release" was created by Dr. Zivorad Slavenski and we have adapted the process here to be used with your Higher Self which releases the trauma cap, stabilizes your energy, and can be used to release the individual emotions quickly and permanently. As with each of the methods of emotion processing in this book, all of these can be self applied, or may be guided by a second party. Performing these methods with the help of your Higher Self is always the most efficient way to do the work.

To determine if you have a trauma(s) and if this method is recommended by your Higher Self for you at this time, do the following:

As described in Chapter Two situate your self either sitting or standing as you have done in the past. Find a quiet place and take control of your mind by finding stillness. Extend your arm to hold the weight so that your shoulder is on a relative par with the weight.

1. Lift the weight to determine the feel of the weight, and pause.
2. State your name: "My name is (Insert your name)." Pause.
3. Lift the weight observing the feel of the heaviness of the weight.
4. Return the weight to the starting point, relaxing your muscle.
5. State a false name: "My name is (make up a name)." Pause.
6. Lift the weight observing the feel of the heaviness of the weight. There should be a distinctly different feel to the weight with the second (false) lift being distinctly heavier.

If the difference between the two lifts is not distinctly different refer to chapter two for ways to obtain accurate responses from your Higher Self.

7. Say, "My Higher Self is with me." Pause.
8. Lift the weight observing the feel of the heaviness of the weight.
9. Return the weight to the starting point, relaxing your muscle.
10. Say, "My Higher Self is not with me." Pause.
11. Lift the weight observing the feel of the heaviness of the weight.
12. Return the weight to the starting point, relaxing your muscle.

Again a distinctly different heaviness should be clearly felt between the two lifts with the affirmative statement being lighter than the negative statement.

13. Say, "It is your, my Higher Self's, recommendation that I use the Trauma Release method to begin my emotional processing work." Pause.
14. Lift the weight observing the feel of the heaviness of the weight.
15. Return the weight to the starting point, relaxing your muscle.
16. Say, "It is not your, my Higher Self's, recommendation that I use the Trauma Release method to begin my emotional processing work." Pause.
17. Lift the weight observing the feel of the heaviness of the weight.
18. Return the weight to the starting point, relaxing your muscle.

If the reply from your Higher Self is that you should begin by using this method (and it will be for most people) then proceed to learn and implement this method first. Some people will only need to use this method one time and others may use it several hours daily for several months. How you have stored your energy is unique and you must trust that your Higher Self has the big picture and knows how to guide you to healing and Enlightenment.

In our directions we will instruct you to stand, however if you are in a wheel chair it will work equally as well. If you have difficulties with balance or have problems with dizziness you may want to do this in a wheel chair. The position of standing is not important, but it is only the mobility that we seek. Do not over extend your physical abilities, but rather adapt the process to your limitations while conforming to the procedural instructions as closely as possible.

19. From your posture and setting for talking to your Higher Self, ask your Higher Self "May we do some work now?" Lift the weight to confirm your Higher Self's readiness to assist you.

20. If the reply was affirmative, ask your Higher Self "we should not do some work now?" The reply will always be affirmative unless you are not prepared because of emotional upset, drug use, illness, or inability on your part to focus your attention.

21. Close your eyes and ask your Higher Self to "please energize the first thing that I need to work on".

22. Become aware of any and all body sensations that you are feeling within your body's core. These sensations will most likely range from your throat to your perineum and may have a variety of sensations. You may even have a recall of a memory that may, or may not have seemed traumatic for you.

23. When you think you have identified the new or emphasized sensation, confirm with your Higher Self that you have properly identified the sensation by placing your hand on where you think you felt the sensation and asking "is this where you activated this energy?"

24. Lift the weight to obtain a confirmation, and then state the inverse, "this is not where you have energized this energy."

25. If your Higher Self says that you did not properly identify the location, then repeat steps 21 through 24 again, asking your higher Self to make the energizing even stronger this time.

26. When you have properly identified the sensation, close your eyes again and ask your Higher Self to give you an

image to go along with this sensation and then focus your attention on what image appears in your mind's eye. It may not seem to be anything from your present or past, but it is something within your energy system that you have associated with the energy/emotion that you are working on. Use it as best you can. If it isn't clear, make it as clear as possible by intensifying your concentration and proceed. Your energy may be too jumbled to visualize clearly. This will improve as you do the work.

If have tried and tried and just cannot get an image, visualize a color, any color that you choose, and use the color as your image until you are able to begin to visualize the image. Be patient with yourself. You are healing and you will soon be able to do the procedure as specified.

27. As you did with the body sensation, confirm with your higher Self that you have properly seen the image. If you have not, ask them to "give you the image and again" and focus your awareness on what appears in you mind's eye.

28. When you have properly identified the body sensation and image stand with you spine as straight as possible, shoulders back. (Your energy runs up and down your spine and the straighter you can hold your spine the more easily it flows.)

29. With your eyes closed, from your mind's eye, push the image in front of your body. Just make sure that it has cleared your body and you are holding the image as still as possible in front of you. (Don't let it be a movie.) If you cannot hold it still, do the exercise anyway. As you

do the process the energy will calm down and become more still.

30. Take the index finger of your right hand (the left hand or another finger on your right hand will work also) and stick it in the middle of the image you are holding in front of you.

31. Feel the body sensation that your Higher Self has given you. Exaggerate it if you need to, to feel it most intensely. Feel the feeling! See the image!

32. Begin to turn your whole body to the left in a circle. Pull the image with you while keeping it squarely in front of you with your finger still in the middle of it.

33. Complete at least four full revolutions to the left (very important to turn only to the left). Stop and feel for the body sensation and to assess the clarity of the image. If you still feel a strong body sensation then turn more revolutions until the body sensation is gone.

34. When it feels like it is gone, return to the posture to talk to you Higher Self and ask your Higher Self "is the energy from that experience gone?" If the answer is negative, repeat the procedure until you get a definitive affirmation that it is all gone. Don't rely just upon your own feeling because that can be misleading if you have already had a big release but there is some small portion remaining. You want it all gone!

35. Assess how you feel; energy movement within your body, fatigue, memories, emotions, and thoughts.

36. If you feel prepared to go on, ask your Higher Self to "energize the next thing you need to work on" and repeat the procedural steps from 21 to 34.

Continue this work session for as long as you are able. If you are at the beginning of the work you may be able to do only one or two processes, however as you release this energy you will be able to perform longer sessions. How quickly you make progress and heal will be totally up to you and how much time and attention you commit to doing the work. After each work session, ask your Higher Self, "Do you advise that I should continue to use this same process for the next session?"

If the answer is negative then inquire which of the other processes in this book would be most beneficial. If you have developed your ability to see the blackboard and confirm what you saw with the weight, then begin using that process the next time you do your work. If you cannot yet see the blackboard you will need to ask about each process individually by lifting the weight for each one (always ask the inverse question to confirm your answer).

This is important: To conclude the session sit quietly for a moment, again taking hold of your mind with your eyes closed. Visualize a big ball of white light appear above your head. Imagine this ball of white light being pressed down through the top of your head and flowing down your head, neck, shoulders, chest, arms, torso, upper legs, and lower legs all the way to your feet. Then imagine a second ball of white light appearing above your head, even larger than the first. Imagine this too being pressed down through the top of your head and following the same path as the first until it fills your whole body. However, the second ball is larger than the first, so image it expanding beyond the limits of your body to encompass your body in a protective shield of white light. Upon completing this task, open your eyes. You have completed the session.

Take a moment to assess how you feel and what you have done. Consider your current mood and frame of mind and offer gratitude to your Higher Self for their assistance in helping you heal. Offer gratitude to the Creator for the experiences you have had and gratitude for the opportunities they have afforded you.

Note: For some people it may be difficult to keep up with the number of turns while doing the process. Before you begin, locate a light source such as a window or lamp. Know that each time you pass this light source (which will be identifiable with your eyes closed) you have made another revolution.

Many people will feel a great relief after the first process or the first session with subsequent sessions yielding less identifiable results. This is normal. As you continue to do the work the results will "feel" variable with some sessions being more emphatically healing and others somewhat blah. They are all working and your Higher Self is bringing up the things in the order that you need to work on them. Have faith in the process and your Higher Self and keep doing it. Your objective is to not just release one piece of emotional baggage, or even a steamer trunk full just to feel better but to heal completely. Enlightenment is a near total clearing and you can achieve this with diligence and commitment!

Chapter Six

The Choice

The most important thing that we can do in the current lifetime and in the string of lifetimes that comprise our experience in Third Density (our current level of consciousness) is to Polarize. Polarization is a seemingly simple thing to accomplish; but looks are deceiving. The choices for polarization are whether we will be Service to Self (STS) or Service to Others (STO). The choice will determine the path of all of our future progress through our evolution.

To make this choice we must raise our consciousness level (ratio of Consciousness to Intelligent Energy) sufficiently to do so. In order to raise our consciousness level we must begin to unload the emotional baggage which we have accumulated along our journey through evolution to date. Learning the tools with which to accomplish this task expeditiously is what we are learning to do with the methods in this book. Reaching the consciousness level of Enlightenment is well beyond the consciousness level necessary to be able to make the choice, and is actually doing the work of the next level of consciousness. If you commit to diligently work to reach Enlightenment you are essentially agreeing to study ahead of the class. It's more strenuous work and is not required if you are content to remain within the class median.

At the current time only 28% of the population of Earth is anticipated to have sufficient consciousness to be able to make this choice. Of the 28% only 16% is anticipated to choose STO and 12% STS. Whether you have polarized and if you have polarized STO or STS is something you can determine very quickly by asking your Higher Self, or if you are still in need of polarizing.

(Hopefully by now you have actually begun to employ the techniques in Chapter Two and have learned how to talk to your Higher Self, so in the future we will just reference that you do your set up to "prepare to talk to your Higher Self", including the initial questions to establish your preparedness to get good answers.)

Prepare to talk to your Higher Self.

1. I have polarized?
2. I have not polarized?
3. I have polarized Service to Self?
4. I have polarized Service to Others?
5. If you have not polarized ask, "By diligently doing the work of releasing the emotional baggage that I have stored within my energy system, I can garner enough energy to polarize?"
6. This is not the case.
7. It is in your plan for me to polarize in this lifetime.
8. It is not in your plan for me to polarize in this lifetime.
9. You (my Higher Self) can and will help me do this?
10. You (my Higher Self) cannot help me do this?

Always conclude a session by offering gratitude to your Higher Self.

Polarizing has little or nothing to do with making an intellectual decision of choosing STS or STO other than as a declaration of your intent. Polarization is measured by both thought and deed and is evident by how you live your life. If you run around "doing" things for others but still harbor emotional baggage that causes you to feel resentment or are not sincere, you may be either still un-polarized or polarized other than what you think you are. The criteria is your true energy system and, unless you are one of the few people that can see another's energy (and even then sufficiently evolved to properly assess it), this is something that only your Higher Self will be able to guide you on.

Making the choice actually becomes somewhat mechanical when you begin to look at it from an energy perspective. We (our individual and cumulative mind/body/spirit complex) are completely energy, including our consciousness. We begin evolution with a very low level of consciousness/energy and simultaneously burden our energy system with our emotional baggage. We begin to amalgamate consciousness so that we are seemingly in a pattern of taking two steps forward and one step back. This continues until we reach a break point (awakening) where we are able to slow and then stop taking on more emotional baggage, begin to unload the emotional baggage we have collected, beginning to amalgamate a greater ratio of consciousness/Intelligent Energy.

One of the primary differences between a STO and a STS individual (mind/body/spirit complex) is that a STO reaches a level of sufficient consciousness where they are able to generate their own energy. A STS individual is not able to generate its own energy, even though it appears to be gaining additional consciousness/energy. Rather than becoming an energy generator the STS individual becomes an increasingly efficient thief of consciousness/energy from other beings. STS must garner, by whatever means possible, energy (consciousness) from STO and other STS that are not as proficient at steeling energy (consciousness). Hence you have the perpetuation of polarity into higher levels of consciousness with ever increasing abilities of STO to generate their own energy by aligning and merging with the Creator, and ever increasing skill of advancing STS in stealing energy from other less skilled STS and STO.

STO feels the pain and suffering (the catalyst) of the emotional baggage that they have accumulated. As a result of the pain and suffering they choose to do the work and unload the emotional baggage. STS opts to not feel the pain and suffering of the emotional baggage but rather opts to suppress it by stealing more and more consciousness/energy by becoming more proficient at the practice, all the while accumulating more emotional baggage. It would seem for the STS that their method would be much like running from the incoming tsunami tide. The faster you run, the faster the tide rolls in and only the individuals able to steal enough consciousness/energy from the others is able to stay ahead of the flooding.

But, as long as you stay ahead of the tide you don't have to go into the emotional baggage that you are carrying. Life/evolution is good as long as you keep running faster and faster. That is one of the primary distinctions between STS and STO. STS refuses to go in and look at the emotional baggage and STO decides to go in and get rid of it. You can't run forever and eventually, in order to finish evolution and unit with the Creator, everyone must go inside and do the work, and this does happen eventually.

Making the choice comes down to whether or not the catalyst of pain and suffering is sufficient to cause you to go inside and do the work now, or whether you choose to keep running in front of the tsunami at the expense of the others you must steal the energy from. In most cases people that have not yet chosen remain uncommitted until "the pain of staying the same is greater than the pain of change." Many people, about 12% of the population of the planet, have made the opposite choice, to become more proficient at stealing energy from others.

Prior to birth, those who have chosen the STS path, plan lives that will support that choice by planning lives of ease and lack of pain and suffering. We recently have identified the collective and refer to these people as the 1% who control most of the wealth, for the most part attend the better schools, run our corporations, religions, governments, etc. It is not absolute that all of these institutional structures are exclusively STS, but you can ask your Higher Self to help you identify who specifically or which bodies of people collectively are polarized STS.

STS is the path of separation from the Creator regardless of what one may intellectualize or vocalize. In order to become a better thief of energy to advance your own cause you must dominate others. You must create hierarchies of structure that raise the most proficient at the theft of energy and domination of others to the top of the hierarchy. Refusal to examine and remove the emotional baggage, as well as the predisposition of domination of others without remorse, guides one to the life of ease where you continue to avoid the catalyst that would cause you to awaken.

If you will recall from the earlier chapters, behavior is determined by our consciousness. Consciousness is not determined by our behavior. Individual behavior is merged into cumulative behavior, so you have segments of the population, brought together by a common bond to steal energy from other groups of people, dominating other groups of people by physical force, intellect, military, finances, religion and all of the other social structures that are prevalent in our world today. If there is the intent to establish an elite by any means there is evidence of the objective of domination of others with the sole spiritual intent of stealing energy to enhance their own advancement at the expense of the others.

Since STS cannot generate their own energy and the energy requires a constant flow, it is not something that one can store and sit on their laurels once achieving a certain quantity of energy. Evolution is a system in motion and it requires a constant flow of energy, so the process of stealing energy becomes a never ending need for more energy, competition, and jockeying for position just to maintain status quo. As STS become more efficient in its theft of energy and needs ever more energy the work to do so become ever more demanding of ruthless behavior.

STS is equally a part of the Creator as the STO. The Creator shows no favoritism to STO just because we, from an STO perspective, may deem it more desirable. Both and STS and STO provide opportunities for the Creator to know itself, so STS in its most dastardly work, is fulfilling the purpose of creation itself.

Admittedly, I am biased towards STO, but with the understanding that STS is a very valuable part of our experience and without it, STO couldn't exist either. Because those who have polarized STS are as much a part of the Creator as STO, STS should be afforded the same universal love and compassion as we would towards any other part of the Creator who experiences the evolutionary process. This is often times very difficult, but integrating the parts into the whole is the process we have undertaken with the evolutionary journey and one which we must fulfill to move forward. As our consciousness escalates we will be able to do this.

STO would seem to be at the mercy of the STS, but just the opposite is true. Remember, we told you that STS is the path of separation even though they seem to be organized into groups? The groups are structures of hierarchy and designed to provide control and pipelines or channels of transportation to the top of the hierarchy to deliver the required energy. Think of the structures of hierarchy as I.V. tubes that are providing a direct transfusion of energy from your arm to the arm at the top of the hierarchy. The more consciousness/energy you gain on the STS path, the more solitary you must become. There is no help along the STS path because that is the nature of the path. However, all you need to do to halt the drain along the I.V. tube is unplug it and you do this by raising your awareness, consciousness, and healing yourself.

The STO path is the path of unity, the path of reunification with the Creator, so there is all the help that you could ever possibly want or need. STS must rely upon direct force (at the lower levels of consciousness) and indirect force at the higher levels. As Dr. Hawkins explains in his book "Power v Force", basic physics dictates any force causes an equal and opposite force to occur. However, power does not create an equal and opposite power (what you tap into when you align with the Creator), and over comes all force, because all elements of creation are one, indivisible from the Creator. It is infinite and it is the "Law of One".

Chapter Seven

Moving Emotion/Energy

The next method of clearing your emotions/energy comprising your emotional baggage is a simple method adapted from a process created by Robert Ducharme and George Rassmussen which we call "Moving Emotion/Energy". If your Higher Self has directed you here for the next method to use in working on releasing your emotional baggage then please read on. Of course you can read on anyway, even if your Higher Self didn't send you here next.

To confirm that your Higher Self has sent you to this method as the next one that will be most effective for you, inquire as follows:

Prepare to talk to your Higher Self.

> a. "It is your (Higher Self) intent for me to use Moving Emotion/Energy as the next method for removing the emotional baggage which I have stored."
> b. "It is not your intent for me to use Moving Emotion/Energy as the next method for removing the emotional baggage which I have stored."
> c. "This method will be most helpful to me at this time for the manner in which I have stored this emotional baggage."
> d. "This method will not be most helpful to me at this time for the manner in which I have stored this emotional baggage."
> e. "You will guide me in my use of this method."
> f. "You will not guide me in my use of this method."

g. "I should continue to use this method until you advise me to move on to the next method."

h. "I should not continue to use this method until you advise me to move on to the next method."

Always offer gratitude to your Higher Self at the completion of each session.

When you are preparing to conduct a work session find a quiet place where you will not be interrupted for the term of the session. You should be alert and well rested and free from any alcohol, drugs, or medications that may hinder your ability to focus. (If you are on prescription medication such as a muscle relaxer, mood stabilizer, or antidepressant the results may be slowed when compare to a person not on these medications, but the processes will still work.) Locate a chair that is comfortable, but not so comfortable that you will sink back into the chair. The chair should have a straight back so that your spine will remain relatively straight during the session.

Prepare to talk to your Higher Self.

1. Ask your Higher Self, "May we conduct a work session now?"

2. Ask your Higher Self, "It would not be good to conduct a work session now?"

If your Higher Self replies in the positive, then proceed.

3. Ask your Higher Self to, "Please energize the next thing I need to work on."

4. After asking this, feel within your body where you feel energy movement. This may be anything from a subtle rumbling sensation or it may be an actual pain. It may

also be in the form of a memory that has strong emotions with it. Whatever it is, use it as long as you can feel the emotion and/or body sensation.

5. When you feel the sensation, place your hand on the sensation and ask your Higher Self "is this where you have energized this energy?"

6. Then ask, "This is not where you have energized this energy?"

7. If the response is positive, then proceed. If the response is negative then ask them to energize the energy again and repeat steps 4 through 6 until you locate what your Higher Self has energized.

8. When you have located the proper location, in your minds eye look at the sensation. Feel the feeling and the emotion associated with that sensation. You may literally ask yourself "what is the emotion that is associated with this body sensation?" Be aware of what the response is.

9. Once you have identified the emotion (if you cannot identify it then proceed anyway), in your mind's eye, look at the sensation and ask yourself the following questions:
   a. "What shape does it have?"
   b. "What color is it?"
   c. "Does it have a texture?" (Rough, smooth, gaseous like, etc.)
   d. "How long does it feel like it has been there?"
   e. "How deep does it feel?"
   f. "Does it feel like it has energy movement within it?"

10. Once you have clearly identified the body sensation /emotion in this way, in your mind's eye, push the

object you have identified in front of and away from your body. (Make sure it clears your body.)

11. Be careful because the object may want to go back inside, but don't permit it to do so.
12. Now, move the object behind you.
13. Then move it above your head.
14. Move it below your feet.
15. Move it to the right of you.
16. Move it to the left of you.
17. Now leave the object outside of you, but return your attention back inside of you and begin a scan in the area where you located this body sensation initially.
18. Search for anything that feels similar to this emotion or body sensation.
19. If you find anything, like scraping crumbs off of the table with your hand, scrap all of the remaining emotion/body sensation into a pile. (You may have to scrape hard to get it out.)
20. Roll this new found energy into a ball and push it outside of you, adding it to the original object that you have already been working with. You may increase the size of the original object to accommodate the addition of the new emotion/energy.
21. Now push the object in front of you, but farther away this time.
22. Push it behind you equal distance.
23. Push it above your head equal distance.
24. Push it below your feet the same distance.
25. Push it to the right of you equal distance.
26. Then, push it to the left of you equal distance.

27. Leave the object outside of you again return your attention inside your body to the same location that you first began.
28. Search for any remaining energy emotion that feels even vaguely similar to what you have been working on.
29. If/when you find anything, with your hands and in your mind's eye, scrap any remaining energy/emotion into a pile, getting everything that you can from inside your body.
30. Roll this remaining energy/emotion into a ball and push this too outside of you and add it to the object you have been working with.
31. Again, push the object in front of you, but this time push it to the horizon, making it a small speck far away from you.
32. Push it behind you to the horizon.
33. Push it above your head to the stratosphere.
34. Push it below your feet to the center of the earth.
35. Push it to the right of you to the horizon.
36. Push it to the left of you to the horizon. As it reaches its maximum distance to the left of you, watch it descending into the earth, never to be seen again.
37. Ask the earth to transmute this energy for you.
38. Return your attention to the place within you that you started from and feel if you can detect anything left of this energy/emotion.
39. Ask your Higher Self, "Did we successfully remove all of this energy/emotion?"
40. Ask your Higher Self, "Did we not successfully remove all of this energy/emotion?"
41. If the answer is negative, repeat the procedure from the beginning. The energy should be worked upon until

your Higher Self gives you the confirmation that "all" of the energy is gone.

42. If the answer is positive, ask your Higher Self to energize the next thing you need to work on and repeat the procedure with this new body sensation from step 4.

This is important: To conclude the session sit quietly for a moment, again taking hold of your mind with your eyes closed. Visualize a big ball of white light appear above your head. Imagine this ball of white light being pressed down through the top of your head and flowing down your head, neck, shoulders, chest, arms, torso, upper legs, and lower legs all the way to your feet. Then imagine a second ball of white light appearing above your head, even larger than the first. Imagine this too being pressed down through the top of your head and following the same path as the first until it fills your whole body. However, the second ball is larger than the first, so image it expanding beyond the limits of your body to encompass your body in a protective shield of white light. Upon completing this task, open your eyes. You have completed the session.

Take a moment to assess how you feel and what you have done. Consider your current mood and frame of mind and offer gratitude to your Higher Self for their assistance in helping you heal. Offer gratitude to the Creator for the experiences you have had and gratitude for the opportunities they have afforded you.

Chapter Eight

Dissolving Emotions/Energy

We will now present you with the next method to remove emotional baggage which has been adapted from a process created by Dr. Zivorad Slavenski originally named "Transcendence", which with adaptations we call "Dissolving Emotion/Energy". If your Higher Self has directed you here for the next method to use in working on removing your emotional baggage then please read on. Of course, as always, you can read on anyway even if your Higher Self didn't send you here next.

To confirm that your Higher Self has sent you to this method as the next one that will be most effective for you, inquire as follows:

Prepare to talk to your Higher Self.

    a.   With the assistance of the weight, make the statement; "it is your (Higher Self) intent for me to use Dissolving Emotion/Energy as the next method for removing the emotional baggage which I have stored."

    b.   With the assistance of the weight, make the statement; "it is not your intent for me to use Dissolving Emotion/Energy as the next method for removing the emotional baggage which I have stored."

    c.   With the assistance of the weight ,make the statement; "this method will be most helpful to me at this time for the manner in which I have stored this emotional baggage."

    d.   With the assistance of the weight, make the statement; "this method will not be most helpful to me at this time for the manner in which I have stored this emotional baggage."

    e. With the assistance of the weight, make the statement; "you will guide me in my use of this method."

    f. With the assistance of the weight, make the statement; "you will not guide me in my use of this method."

    g. With the assistance of the weight, make the statement; "I should continue to use this method until you advise me to move on to the next method."

    h. With the assistance of the weight, make the statement; "I should not continue to use this method until you advise me to move on to the next method."

Always offer gratitude to your Higher Self at the completion of each session.

When you are preparing to conduct a work session find a quiet place where you will not be interrupted for the term of the session. You should be alert and well rested and free from any alcohol, drugs, or medications that may hinder your ability to focus. (If you are on prescription medication such as a muscle relaxer, mood stabilizer, or antidepressant the results may be slowed when compare to a person not on these medications, but the processes will still work.) Locate a chair that is comfortable, but not so comfortable that you will sink back into the chair. The chair should have a straight back so that your spine will remain relatively straight during the session.

Prepare to talk to your Higher Self.

1. Close your eyes and keep them closed until you are finished with the session.
2. With the assistance of the weight, ask your Higher Self; "May we conduct a work session now?"

3. With the assistance of the weight, ask your Higher Self; "It would not be good to conduct a work session now?"

If your Higher Self replies in the positive, then proceed.

4. Ask your Higher Self to please, "Energize the next thing I need to work on."
5. After asking this, feel within your body where you feel energy movement and/or a body sensation (maybe a tightening, rumbling feeling, or anything new that emerges or intensifies after you ask). This may be a subtle sensation or it may be intense. It may also be in the form of a memory that evokes emotions or seems to be located within a certain area of the body. Whatever it is, use it as long as you can feel the emotion and/or body sensation.
6. When you feel the sensation, place your hand on the sensation and with the assistance of the weight, ask your Higher Self; "is this where you have energized this energy?"
7. Then make the statement, with the assistance of the weight; "this is not where you have energized this energy?"
8. If the response is positive, then proceed. If the response is negative then ask them to energize the energy again and repeat steps 4 through 6 until you locate what your Higher Self has energized.
9. When you have located the proper location look at the sensation. Feel the feeling and the emotion associated with that sensation. You may literally ask yourself "what is the emotion that is associated with this body sensation?" Be aware of what the response is.

10. Once you have identified the feeling (if you cannot identify the emotion proceed anyway), in your mind's eye, look at the sensation and ask yourself the following questions:
    a. "What shape does it have?"
    b. "What color is it?"
    c. "Does it have a texture?" (Rough, smooth, gaseous like, etc.)
    d. "How long does it feel like it has been there?"
    e. "How deep does it feel?"
    f. "Does it feel like it has energy movement within it?"
11. Once you have identified the body sensation /emotion in this way, in your mind's eye, push the object you have defined in front of and away from your body. (Make sure it clears your body.)
12. Be careful here because the object may want to go back inside, but don't permit it to do so.
13. With the object held in front of you, visualize an angel (or other positive image) appearing in your periphery vision on the <u>right side</u>.
14. Ask the angel to move in front of you and position itself between you and the object.
15. Begin breathing into the angel.
16. As you continue to visualize your breath/energy moving into the angel, see the angel slowly beginning to glow a golden light.
17. As you continue to breathe into the angel, see the angel begin to glow brighter and bright, beginning to pulse and radiate golden energy.

18. Continue to breathe into the angel until you can feel the warm comforting energy radiating over your face, neck, and chest.

19. When the golden light is so bright that you cannot see anything but the light from the angel, hold that vision until the body sensation that you began with dissolves.

20. Once you can no longer feel the body sensation, ask the angel to move back over to the right side.

21. Return your attention to the place within you that you started from and feel if you can detect anything left of this energy/emotion.

22. With the assistance of the weight, ask your Higher Self; "did we successfully remove all of this energy/emotion?"

23. With the assistance of the weight, ask your Higher Self; "did we not successfully remove all of this energy/emotion?"

24. If the answer is negative, ask the angel to again position itself between you and the object and begin breathing into the angel again, repeating the process. The energy should be worked upon until your Higher Self gives you the confirmation that "all" of the energy is gone.

25. If the answer is positive, ask your Higher Self to energize the next thing you need to work on and repeat the procedure with this new body sensation from step 4.

26. Before you leave the session inquire of your Higher Self, with the assistance of the weight, if you should stay with this method for the next session, or should move on to another method of clearing your emotional baggage.

This is important: To conclude the session sit quietly for a moment, again taking hold of your mind with your eyes closed.

Visualize a big ball of white light appear above your head. Imagine this ball of white light being pressed down through the top of your head and flowing down your head, neck, shoulders, chest, arms, torso, upper legs, and lower legs all the way to your feet. Then imagine a second ball of white light appearing above your head, even larger than the first. Imagine this too being pressed down through the top of your head and following the same path as the first until it fills your whole body. However, the second ball is larger than the first, so imagine it expanding beyond the limits of your body to encompass your body in a protective shield of white light. Upon completing this task, open your eyes. You have completed the session.

Take a moment to assess how you feel and what you have done. Consider your current mood and frame of mind and offer gratitude to your Higher Self for their assistance in helping you heal. Offer gratitude to the Creator for the experiences you have had and gratitude for the opportunities they have afforded you.

Chapter Nine

Integrating Polarities

The next method to remove emotional baggage was created by Dr. Zivorad Slavenski and is named "Basic PEAT". "PEAT" is an acronym for "Prime Energy Activation and Transcendence". If your Higher Self has directed you here for the next method to use in working on removing your emotional baggage then please read on. Learning and using all of these methods simply adds more arrows in your quiver to be able to aid yourself and others.

Emotions are selected based upon the resonance of our internal vibration at any given moment/experience with the resonance of the energy of the experience. If our vibration is very low at the time, we will select a very low vibration to associate with the experience. If our vibration is very high at the time, we will use that vibration to associate with the experience. We perceive this behavior to be a polarity of high vibration v low vibration when actually it is only different ends of the same scale completely connected; one end with the other. However, since we "perceive" it to be a polarity we can use methods of integrating the two perceived polarities into a position of neutrality, or, in other words, "take the charge off of the emotion".

In this simple exercise we are integrating perceptions/feelings with the left and right hemispheres of the brain, each of which has a different vibrational perception. It is very important that we "feel" (not think) about the emotions. Thinking about integrating or releasing them will cause them to persist.

To confirm that your Higher Self has sent you to this method as the next one that will be most effective, inquire as follows:

Prepare to talk to your Higher Self.

a. "It is your (Higher Self) intent for me to use Basic PEAT as the next method for removing the emotional baggage which I have stored."

b. "It is not your intent for me to use Basic PEAT as the next method for removing the emotional baggage which I have stored."

c. "This method will be most helpful to me at this time for the manner in which I have stored this emotional baggage."

d. "This method will not be most helpful to me at this time for the manner in which I have stored this emotional baggage."

e. "You will guide me in my use of this method."

f. "You will not guide me in my use of this method."

g. "I should continue to use this method until you advise me to move on to the next method."

h. "I should not continue to use this method until you advise me to move on to the next method."

Always offer gratitude to your Higher Self at the completion of each session.

When you are preparing to conduct a work session find a quiet place where you will not be interrupted for the term of the session. You should be alert and well rested and free from any alcohol, drugs, or medications that may hinder your ability to focus. (If you are on prescription medication such as a muscle relaxer, mood stabilizer, or antidepressant the results may be slowed when compared to a person not on these medications, but the processes will still work.) Locate a chair that is comfortable, but not so comfortable that you will sink back into the chair. The chair should have a straight back so that your spine will remain relatively straight during the session.

Prepare to talk to your Higher Self.

1. Close your eyes and keep them closed until you are finished with the session.
2. Ask your Higher Self, "May we conduct a work session now?"
3. Ask your Higher Self, "It would not be good to conduct a work session now?"

If your Higher Self replies in the positive, then proceed.

4. With the assistance of the weight, ask your Higher Self to please, "Energize the next thing I need to work on."
5. After asking this, feel within your body where you feel energy movement or body sensation (which is energy movement). This may be a subtle sensation or it may be an actual pain. It may also be in the form of a memory that has a location and/or emotion and body sensation too. Whatever it is, use it as long as you can feel the emotion and/or body sensation.
6. When you feel the sensation, place your hand on the sensation and ask your Higher Self, with the assistance of the weight, "is this where you have energized this energy?"
7. With the assistance of the weight, then ask, "This is not where you have energized this energy?"
8. If the response is positive, then proceed. If the response is negative then ask them to energize the energy again

and repeat steps 4 through 6 until you locate what your Higher Self has energized.

9. When you have confirmed the proper location look at the sensation. Feel the feeling and the emotion associated with that sensation. You may literally ask yourself "what is the emotion that is associated with this body sensation?" Be aware of what the response is. It is not necessary to know the emotion to proceed.

10. Once you have identified the emotion (if you cannot identify it then proceed anyway), but feel the feeling (emotion and/or body sensation) as intensely as you can.

11. Place the first two fingers of your dominant hand over the top of your chest plate about three inches down from the bottom of the "U" at the base of your throat.

12. Say this statement: "Even though I feel (fear, heart brokenness, shame, etc.; if you cannot identify the emotion, describe body sensation and/or the location within your body, ie. "pain in my chest"), I deeply love and accept myself, my body and personality, and the fact that I feel this (repeat the emotion or body sensation you are working on).

13. Place the first two fingers of the left hand on the left side of your face where the bridge of the nose meets the ocular bone. (Below the interior end of the eyebrow.)

14. <u>Feel the feeling as intensely as you can</u>, focusing all your attention on this location that your Higher Self has energized for you. Exaggerate the feeling if you need to so that you feel it deeply and completely. Be patient with yourself and allow the feeling to come to the surface.

15. When you are feeling it as intensely as you think you can, inhale a deep breath and slowly exhale. The breath is important so don't hurry through it. This is what actually moves the energy.

16. Now take the first two fingers of the right hand and place them on the right side of your face on the mirrored location of your first position.

17. Feel the feeling as intensely as you can, focusing all your attention on this location that your Higher Self has energized for you. Exaggerate the feeling if you need to so you can feel it deeply and completely. Be patient with yourself and allow the feeling to come to the surface.

18. When you are feeling it as intensely as you think you can, inhale a deep breath and slowly exhale.

19. Place the first two fingers of the left hand on the left side of your face outside of the eye on the ocular bone.

20. Feel the feeling as intensely as you can, focusing all your attention on this location that your Higher Self has energized for you. Exaggerate the feeling if you need to so you can feel it deeply and completely. Be patient with yourself and allow the feeling to come to the surface.

21. When you are feeling it as intensely as you think you can, inhale a deep breath and slowly exhale.

22. Now take the first two fingers of the right hand and place them on the right side of your face on the mirrored location of left side position.

23. Feel the feeling as intensely as you can, focusing all your attention on this location that your Higher Self has energized for you. Exaggerate the feeling if you need to so you can feel it deeply and completely. Be patient

with yourself and allow the feeling to come to the surface.

24. When you are feeling it as intensely as you think you can, inhale a deep breath and slowly exhale.

25. Place the first two fingers of the left hand on the left side of your face centered under the eye on the ocular bone.

26. <u>Feel the feeling as intensely as you can</u>, focusing all your attention on this location that your Higher Self has energized for you. Exaggerate the feeling if you need to so you can feel it deeply and completely. Be patient with yourself and allow the feeling to come to the surface.

27. When you are feeling it as intensely as you think you can, inhale a deep breath and slowly exhale.

28. Take the first two fingers of the right hand and place them on the right side of your face on the mirrored location of left side position.

29. <u>Feel the feeling as intensely as you can</u>, focusing all your attention on this location that your Higher Self has energized for you. Exaggerate the feeling if you need to so you can feel it deeply and completely. Be patient with yourself and allow the feeling to come to the surface.

30. When you are feeling it as intensely as you think you can, inhale a deep breath and slowly exhale.

31. Return your attention to the place within you that you started from and feel if you can detect anything remaining of this energy/emotion.

32. With the assistance of the weight, ask your Higher Self, "Did we successfully remove all of this energy/emotion?"

33. With the assistance of the weight, ask your Higher Self, "Did we not successfully remove all of this energy/emotion?"
34. If the answer is positive, ask your Higher Self to energize the next thing you need to work on and repeat the procedure with this new body sensation from step 5.
35. Before you leave the session inquire of your Higher Self , with the assistance of the weight, if you should stay with this method for the next session, or should move on to another method of clearing your emotional baggage.

This is important: To conclude the session sit quietly for a moment, again taking hold of your mind with your eyes closed. Visualize a big ball of white light appear above your head. Imagine this ball of white light being pressed down through the top of your head and flowing down your head, neck, shoulders, chest, arms, torso, upper legs, and lower legs all the way to your feet. Then imagine a second ball of white light appearing above your head, even larger than the first. Imagine this too being pressed down through the top of your head and following the same path as the first until it fills your whole body. However, the second ball is larger than the first, so image it expanding beyond the limits of your body to encompass your body in a protective shield of white light. Upon completing this task, open your eyes. You have completed the session.

Take a moment to assess how you feel and what you have done. Consider your current mood and frame of mind and offer gratitude to your Higher Self for their assistance in helping you heal. Offer gratitude to the Creator for the experiences you have had and gratitude for the opportunities they have afforded you.

Chapter Ten

Bodhisattva Enlightenment

In this section we will offer the final method for removing emotional baggage from your energy system. We have called this method the Bodhisattva Enlightenment method because it is the most simple method, and yet it is the most difficult to perform for most people. This method is listed last on the list because it is the last method anyone will need. This is the one that will carry you over the finish line. You will be directed to this method by your Higher Self at the appropriate time. It is important that you follow the direction of your Higher Self as to which method to use, because they are the ones that know where and how you have stored the baggage and, while you may think yourself able to do this method you will miss some things that other methods presented earlier may be more efficient in unloading.

There is no pride, only ego, in going to this method before you are ready. In fact, pride is an emotion that will need some serious work too. Learning to surrender to the direction of your Higher Self is part of the process of working towards Enlightenment. As long as you cling to old habits of "turning your own wheel of fate" you will be thwarted in your desires for Enlightenment.

We have named this method Bodhisattva Enlightenment because it is this method that will propel you over the top. This method allows you to do wholesale work according to your willingness to surrender to your Higher Self. It is the method used by Siddhartha Gautama (AKA The Blessed One, The

Buddha, etc.) There is no end to the healing work that you can accomplish with this simple method, and no end to the awareness that is made available to you as a result of continued and diligent application.

The method was taught to me by Judith Daniel, a student and protégée of Dr. Zivorad Slavenski and practitioner and teacher of his methods. It has been here adapted to incorporate the guidance of your Higher Self which makes it more complete.

As we have already discussed, emotions are nothing more than a range of vibrating energy and emotional baggage is composed of clumps of this similarly vibrating energy that we have stored/stuck within our energy system. It is our perceptions and/or interpretation of our experiences that cause us to choose one rate of vibrating energy over another (AKA one emotion over another). Releasing the clumps of lower vibrating energy becomes a matter of raising the vibration rate of the lower energy by removing the bonds that hold it in place.

To confirm that your Higher Self has sent you to this method as the next one that will be most effective, inquire as follows:

Prepare to talk to your Higher Self.

   a.   "It is my Higher Self's intent for me to use the
        Bodhisattva Enlightenment as the next method for
        removing the emotional baggage which I have stored."
   b.   "It is not your intent for me to use the Bodhisattva
        Enlightenment as the next method for removing the
        emotional baggage which I have stored."
   c.   "This method will be most helpful to me at this time for
        the manner in which I have stored this emotional
        baggage."

d. "This method will not be most helpful to me at this time for the manner in which I have stored this emotional baggage."
e. "You will guide me in the use of this method."
f. "You will not guide me in the use of this method."

Always offer gratitude to your Higher Self at the completion of each session.

When you are preparing to conduct a work session find a quiet place where you will not be interrupted for the term of the session. You should be alert and well rested and free from any alcohol, drugs, or medications that may hinder your ability to focus. (If you are on prescription medication such as a muscle relaxer, mood stabilizer, or antidepressant the results may be slowed when compared to a person not on these medications, but the processes will still work.) Locate a chair that is comfortable, but not so comfortable that you will sink back into the chair. The chair should have a straight back so that your spine will remain relatively straight during the session.

Prepare to talk to your Higher Self.

1. Close your eyes and keep them closed until you are finished with the session.
2. Ask your Higher Self, "May we conduct a work session now?"
3. Ask your Higher Self, "It would not be good to conduct a work session now?"

If your Higher Self replies in the positive, then proceed.

4. Take hold of your mind and focus your attention on your sixth Chakra (Indigo Ray energy, Form Maker

Chakra, Third Eye Chakra), located at the center of your brow. Hold this focus until you can feel the energy movement at this location.

5. When you can feel this energy movement, and with the assistance of the weight, ask your Higher Self, "am I prepared to do work now?"

6. If the answer is negative, return your attention to the sixth Chakra and continue to hold your focus and attention here until you can more clearly feel this energy and then repeat the question in step 5.

7. When you get a positive reply from your Higher Self, ask your Higher Self to energize the next thing you need to work on, and then bring your awareness inside your body. Observe any energy movement and/or body sensation that you may feel in your core.

8. When you have identified an energy movement and/or body sensation, place your hand on the location and ask your Higher Self, with the assistance of the weight, if this is the proper location.

9. If the reply is negative, repeat the procedure in step 8.

10. When you get a positive reply, ask for the name of this emotion (fear, shame, guilt, grief, etc.) When you think you have heard (or just know) the emotion, with the assistance of the weight, ask your Higher Self if this is the proper emotion. It will be helpful, but not necessary if you have not already learned to do so, to identify the emotion in future processing sessions.

11. Once you have the location and name of the lower vibration energy (emotion) and can clearly "feel" it, return your attention to the sixth Chakra and cause the "feeling" of the higher vibration sixth Chakra energy to

move down, adjacent to the feeling of the lower vibration energy.

12. It is important that you do not "make" them do anything, but just hold the higher vibration adjacent to the lower vibration and allow them to experience each other. (To just "be" next to each other.)

13. Hold the feeling of the two vibrations together (side by side, or over and under) until the lower vibration goes away, or until the feeling of the vibration substantially changes. This may be quickly experienced, or may take several minutes.

14. With the assistance of the weight, ask your Higher Self; "is the energy from that emotion fully integrated/gone?"

15. If the reply is negative, begin at step 4 again.

16. If the reply is positive, ask your Higher Self to; "please energize the next thing I need to work on" and begin again from step 7.

17. You should not need to re-energize the higher vibration energy each time.

18. In order to assist in your concentration of feeling the two vibrations you may want to assign a color to the higher vibration sixth Chakra energy and a different color to the lower vibration energy and visualize the two colors being held next to each other. Never substitute the color for the feeling. Only use the color to augment your concentration of the two feelings coming together. When the color changes or the lower vibration goes away, ask your Higher Self the question in step 14.

19. As you develop your skill and comfort with this method you should be able to move from sensation to sensation

without checking each one to see if it is removed or to invite your Higher Self to energize each one individually. Your Higher Self will quickly move you from one to the other, allowing you to hold the higher vibration to the lower one until it is gone before introducing the next location to work on.

20. When your skill and improved communication with your Higher Self allows you to work as described in step 19 you will want to inquire, at the conclusion of the session, if you were successful in removing all of the emotions worked on by asking, with the assistance of the weight, "were we successful in removing all of the energy in all of the locations that we worked on in this session?" the reply should be positive, but if not, ask to revisit whatever you did not complete before departing the session.

This is important: To conclude the session sit quietly for a moment, again taking hold of your mind with your eyes closed. Visualize a big ball of white light appear above your head. Imagine this ball of white light being pressed down through the top of your head and flowing down your head, neck, shoulders, chest, arms, torso, upper legs, and lower legs all the way to your feet. Then imagine a second ball of white light appearing above your head, even larger than the first. Imagine this too being pressed down through the top of your head and following the same path as the first until it fills your whole body. However, the second ball is larger than the first, so image it expanding beyond the limits of your body to encompass your body in a protective shield of white light. Upon completing this task, open your eyes. You have completed the session.

Take a moment to assess how you feel and what you have done. Consider your current mood and frame of mind and offer gratitude to your Higher Self for their assistance in helping you heal. Offer gratitude to the Creator for the experiences you have had and gratitude for the opportunities they have afforded you.

Chapter Eleven

Meditation

As introduced in the earlier sections of these writings, we currently enjoy the experience of Third Density on our evolutionary journey. This density is characterized by a range of consciousness, on either side of which is another density of experience, one higher with a corresponding greater ratio of Consciousness to Intelligent Energy, and one lower with a greater ratio of Intelligent Energy to Consciousness. We who are in the Third Density on earth at this time, as is characteristic of all Third Density experiences, are possessed of 100% of the potential consciousness of this experience. Most of us are using the major portion of this consciousness/energy to carry the emotional baggage that we have collected, thereby making this Consciousness unavailable to us for other more productive things, such as becoming awake and conscious.

When we release the emotional baggage the consciousness/energy previously unavailable to us becomes liberated from this burden and is available to be used for more productive things. This liberated consciousness facilitates our achievement of such things as universal love and enlightenment. It also gives us the capacity to understand who we are and behave in a way more suited to the new found higher Consciousness of our beingness. We begin to do without things like war, enslavement, and fear of non-survival.

One of the other things that consciousness/energy is used for is to live life. In addition to our current requirement to allocate large quantities of energy from our reservoir of

Consciousness/energy to carry/suppress emotional baggage, we use consciousness/energy to think, regulate our sensory input data, and exchange energy with other people in our daily life (AKA our behavior). For most of us even the energy not used to support our emotional baggage is very poorly managed. This is the very nature of chaos and causes the condition of unconsciousness (as the Buddha named it, "ignorance") to almost be self sustaining. We don't have enough energy to fix our lack of energy problem.

Initially, it is through the "strength of our will" to change, from the well established pattern of remaining in pain and suffering (unconsciousness/ignorance) to one of healing, that begins to pull enough Consciousness/energy from the system to begin to do the work. This is the energy necessary to begin to get the ball rolling and permit momentum to become a positive factor. Once you begin to do the work of releasing the emotional baggage, the momentum increases and accelerates. Chaos, even though it may be tough to see, begins to subside and an introductory level of stability begins to appear.

Meditation, the second prong of the process of achieving Enlightenment, is the process of learning to efficiently manage the consciousness/energy, which may be currently available in small quantities, as well as the newly released consciousness/energy that appears as we do the processing work. Meditation does two things; 1) builds concentration, and 2) builds awareness, or in other words, begins to manage our consciousness/energy. In order to achieve Enlightenment it is necessary to embolden the "discipline of the personality" which meditation is designed to do. Discipline of the personality comes from learning to marshal the available consciousness/energy to its most efficacious applications.

Most people find meditation very difficult or impossible to do. Traditionally, the prescription for this difficulty would be too "tough it out" and rely upon the building of the discipline of the personality to improve the meditative practice. However, most people don't have the energy/consciousness to do this. If most of your available consciousness/energy is being used to carry truck loads of emotional baggage the allocation of additional energy to such basic requirements as simple sensory input and living from day to day forces you into overload. You don't have anything left to allocate to disciplining the personality or to meditate. However, as you liberate consciousness/energy by unloading the emotional baggage truck with the process outlined in preceding chapters, meditation becomes much easier to accomplish.

The person who will have the most difficulty beginning the work is the one that is still functional. These people are the stalwarts of middle class; holding a job, participating in family, and to all appearances are "doing fine" (AKA getting by). The person who will most likely be ready to take the plunge and seriously begin to do the work is the one who is suffering the most; the drug addict, the person with a serious diagnosed physical or mental illness, the homeless person, or any other social evidence of extreme chaos and inability to locate any stability. The people in the most suffering are actually closer to Enlightenment because of their motivation to do the work.

Beyond the beginning stages of learning to manage the Consciousness/energy (AKA taking control of the mind), and after gaining additional Consciousness/energy to work with by the liberation methods provided, there are two primary paths of a meditative practice. One path is the passive meditation involving the clearing of the mind and the emptying of the mental jumble and is perfect for those whose goal is to achieve an inner silence as a base from which to listen to the Creator. The other path is a meditation which may be called visualization and has as its goal that which is not contained in the meditation itself. Visualization is the tool of the adept (Enlightened) and has as its goal the consciousness raising of the planetary vibration/consciousness.

One is not mutually exclusive of the other. It is absolutely possible and even probable that a meditator will endeavor to work to achieve both objectives of each meditation path. But to practice either path you have begin to meditate.

Meditation should not be a masochistic exercise. It should be an enjoyable experience that one looks forward to performing and regrets leaving. However, we often set our expectations too high to begin with. Like a desire to run a 26 mile marathon, we set our sites on meditating for an hour or more. We begin to run/meditate and find that after reaching only the end of the block we are wheezing/"watching the clock" and struggling to keep going. As with running, start with what you can do and "push the envelope" just a little more each time you meditate. If you can meditate 5 minutes comfortably, meditate for 6 minutes. If you can meditate for 15 minutes comfortably, push your time on the cushion to 17 minutes. Do it every day, without fail. (Also the emotion processing method that is appropriate for you.) If you allow yourself to negotiate with your mind over whether you have time, energy, or a desire to do something else, you will loose.

We cannot recommend one method of meditation as being better than another. There are dozens of different books on the market offering instruction on meditation and several good centers in most cities (yoga exercise alone doesn't count). Experiment with several until you find a method that works best for you. You will probably seek another method before long that meets the needs of where you are with your practice at that time. That is OK, the point is to meditate. As you unload the emotional baggage your abilities, awareness, and discipline of personality will change with the new consciousness/energy you are experiencing.

We do, however, strongly suggest that you find a guru, instructor, experienced meditator to work with. It is always better to have a resource available to you that has already experienced what you are experiencing and that can guide you more productively to your goal. Of course, your Higher Self is always available and is your best guide, since they traveled this road a long time ago and have coached many others to the finish line. (That's right. You're not the only one.) However, until your communication abilities with your Higher Self improve; find a human to work with.

If you can't find a local meditation instructor or meditation center that you like, we offer the following program to get you started:

1. Find a place that will be your meditation place. This can be a whole room or the corner of your bedroom. Let everyone in the house know that when you are here, you are meditating. This goes for you too. When you are here, you are meditating and nothing else is more important. If you travel and don't have the luxury of a place to go to every time, visualize a special item of clothing (a cloak or cape) and know that when, in your mind, you put on this cloak… you are in meditation.

When you finish, ceremoniously take it off and put it away.

2. Many older traditions specify a very rigorous posture. The best posture is the one that works for you. It is very important that your posture be one that permits your spine to be relatively straight. You can sit in a chair or on the floor, but with spine straight, align your ears over your shoulders. Place your hands comfortably on your thighs, push the lower part of your abdomen slightly forward, and close your eyes.

3. If you are going to sit on the floor we recommend that you invest in a Zafu (cushion of buckwheat filling) and zabuton (mat). The zafu should raise your bottom 4 to 6 inches above the floor height. Cross your legs comfortable. There are a variety of leg positions that may work, but the objective is to form a tri-pod configuration between your two knees and your bottom.

4. Close your eyes and begin by exhaling all of the air from your lungs.

5. Inhale a long deep breath and release it slowly.

6. Again inhale a long deep breath and release it slowly.

7. One more time, inhale a long deep breath and release it slowly.

8. On the next inhale, begin visualizing an egg forming inside of your body. Allow the egg to become fully formed.

9. Begin to visualize a small light beginning to form on the outside of the egg and have it begin to move around the outside of the egg from top to bottom (follow the oval shape).

10. Allow the light moving around the egg to assume a smooth and easy rhythm.

11. Allow your focus and attention to begin following the light around the egg, also conforming to the smooth and easy rhythm.

12. As you focus on the light moving around the egg, notice that your in-breath is connecting to the out-breath, and that your out-breath is connecting to the in-breath. Allow this to happen and it will begin to flow comfortably and naturally as you keep your focus on the light moving around the egg.

13. Allow this breath to stabilize and the smooth rhythm to continue for several minutes.

14. When you are ready, on an out-breath, push the bottom of the egg down to the bottom of your spine (1st Chakra).

15. Continue to follow the light around the egg and to connect the in-breath and the out-breath, still following a smooth and easy rhythm.

16. Allow this breath to stabilize and the smooth rhythm to continue for several minutes.

17. If you have a thought come in to distract you or divert your attention, simply dismiss it and return your attention to the light moving around the egg.

18. When you are ready, on an in-breath, pull the top of the egg up to your brow.

19. Continue to follow the light around the egg and to connect the in-breath and the out-breath, still following a smooth and easy rhythm.

20. Allow this breath to stabilize and the smooth rhythm to continue for several minutes.

21. If you have continuous thoughts come in to distract you or divert your attention, increase the rhythm of your breathing to stabilize your ability to focus on the light.

22. If you find yourself dozing off or in anyway being distracted, return your attention to the light moving around the egg.

23. New meditation students (we are all students, no matter how long we have been doing it) should do this exercise for 15 to 30 minutes twice a day.

24. Choose a time to meditate that you are at your most alert. This should not be a relaxation exercise just before you go to sleep.

You should begin to notice significant changes in your outlook on life and changes within you in as little as two weeks. You can expand this simple exercise by experimenting with different things for the egg to do, such as, extending it a second time below your feet and above your head. Once expanded, you can contract the egg in increments back to its original position. You should use this exercise as a transition tool to take you from your everyday mind to a meditation state before you do more significant work, when you are ready.

The objective of any meditation is to take you inside yourself and to heighten your concentration and awareness. Become aware of what you feel and where; body sensations, emotions, energy movement, etc. Your experience will be your own. The more you learn to focus, the faster the path to Enlightenment will be achieved.

Chapter Twelve

Mind/Body/Spirit Healing

The tools offered in this book can be life changing. Whether or not you reach Enlightenment is entirely up to you, but you now have the tools to do so. It will require commitment and dedication on your part, but it is available in a relatively short period of time. How long a period of time will depend upon you; where you begin, how often and how long per session you work on it, and how willing you are to change (AKA surrender) from who you are to who you can be.

The tools offered here work on your spiritual being. However, we are a mind/body/spirit complex, which means that all three levels of our beingness should be addressed simultaneously. Since the tools offered in this book work on the spirit, you could say that you are working on all three and you would be right. But the spiritual creates the mental and the mental creates the physical. If you wait for the process to work (spiritual > mental > physical) it will take longer for all the changes to filter down to the physical.

We have also pointed out we usually stay the same until the pain of staying the same becomes greater than the pain of change. Based upon this truth we assume that you, the reader, are in some degree of pain or suffering that you want to change, be it physical, emotional, or mental. A unified and balanced approach to healing the mind, the body, and the spirit is going to expedite the process so we will briefly address the mind and body parts of our beingness.

The mental part will change as you do the work in this book. However, working on changing your mental status directly will make it go faster. Establishing a routine, along with the work set forth in earlier chapters will work directly on the mental. You can do this very simply by including in your day a series of positive affirmations. Make note cards for yourself and place them around your home and office where you are likely to focus your attention throughout the day.

These are three of my favorites that have been helpful to me:

"Divine wisdom gently guides me. I offer all problems up to my Higher Self and the way is made smooth and clear." - Unknown

"Infinite Creator, how may I serve the greater good this day? Show me your ways, teach me your ways." – Quo

"I am an infinitely powerful, eternal, immortal creator being." - Avirl

A student recently asked if offering positive affirmations by themselves wouldn't do the same thing as the program outlined in this book. Imagine that you have a half barrel of rotting apples and you want to replace them with good apples. Would you put good apples in the same barrel with the rotting apples, or would you empty the rotting apples out before putting in the good apples? I hope you said that you should empty out the rotting apples before adding the good because it is the same thing with removing the emotional baggage before adding new shinny consciousness to your energy system. (Also, you can ask your Higher Self.)

Learning to "Observe your Thoughts" is another extremely helpful practice to adopt to assist in healing the mind. Traditionally this practice is called "Mindfulness" and is usually associated with the function of meditation. Mindfulness can be practiced within meditation but my preference is to identify mindfulness as the function of taking the awareness that you practice within meditation with you throughout the day.

Regrettably we cannot keep the same amount of our focus and attention on our internal being as we do when in meditation as we go about our day, but we can always be aware if our conscious attention is totally disbursed outside of us. It is ideal if you can arrange a co-reminder system with a friend or spouse to periodically catch each other throughout the day and inquire of each other "where is your awareness". The purpose of this random reminder is to catch you when your attention is disbursed and make you sufficiently aware to bring a portion of your consciousness back inside your being. This means to feel your consciousness inside of you by feeling your heart or feeling where else within you that your consciousness might be lurking. This has proven to be a great tool to assist people in simply becoming aware of where their mind goes as we journey through our day.

Think of your conscious awareness as if it were a clutch on your car. The clutch of awareness serves as a transfer agent for how much awareness you keep inside and how much you allow to go outside. When the surrounding conditions demand, you let the clutch out to release your conscious awareness sufficiently to "deal" with whatever experience you are having. However, when the outside demands lessen, you retrieve your conscious awareness back inside to maintain your grounding and stability. The clutch allows you to feel where your awareness is and to monitor the demands being placed upon your energy/consciousness. This awareness of the point where your consciousness moves in and out is called the friction point. With only a little practice you too will be able to begin to respond to life's energy demands and begin to monitor your energy and consciousness.

If you don't have a friend or spouse to share this co-development exercise set an alarm on your watch or phone so that you can be prompted periodically to be aware of your awareness. When it catches you aware, even partially of your inner self, then pat yourself on the back (figuratively). When it catches you lost in your surroundings then simply focus your awareness inside and rededicate yourself to do better next time. Practice being aware of what is inside and what is outside at the same time.

The other major area of work for most people is to become aware of and change what you put into your body. The body is a delicate instrument and responds almost immediately to bad fuel. If you maintain a typical American diet you are putting bad fuel into your physical vehicle every time you eat. Organic food (formerly called food) offers vital nutrients that your body needs. GMO food is soulless food and offers little of what your body needs. Processed food is, well, just a waste of your effort.

Three common ailments that result in significant hindrance to Enlightenment are heavy metal (not music) toxicity, gluten, and yeast (Candida) overgrowth. Gluten and yeast overgrowth are as a result of poor diets and heavy metal toxicity is a result of absorption of poison in the environment. Any one of which can greatly slow your progress but you can correct each of these conditions with some effort on your part.

You can determine if these, or others conditions, are causing you difficulty by simply asking your Higher Self.

Prepare to talk to your Higher Self.

21. Close your eyes and keep them closed until you are finished with the session.
22. With the assistance of the weight, ask your Higher Self "Will you aid me in some physical diagnostic questions now?"
23. With the assistance of the weight, ask your Higher Self, "You will not aid me in some physical diagnostic questions now?"

If your Higher Self replies in the positive, then proceed.

24. With the assistance of the weight ask, "Do I have heavy metal toxicity?"
25. With the assistance of the weight ask, "Do I not have heavy metal toxicity?"
26. If the reply is positive, with the assistance of the weight ask, "Is this heavy metal mercury?"
27. With the assistance of the weight ask, "Is this heavy metal not mercury?"
28. If the reply is yes that you have heavy metal toxicity but not mercury, then go through a list of possible culprits including cadmium, aluminum, etc. Most physicians are not trained, nor are commonly used tests effective in detecting heavy metals effectively until it reaches extreme levels. It will be necessary to locate a physician that has been specially trained in these areas to work with you on removing this condition.

One of the first and best things you can do immediately if you have amalgam fillings in your teeth is to have the fillings removed and replaced with a non-toxic substitute. However, do not go to your local dentist and have them popped out. It will require removal by a specially trained dentist that knows how to remove them without releasing a burst of mercury into your system in the removal process. When you find one that appears to have the proper training, ask your Higher Self if he/she (the dentist) does in fact have the training necessary. (Better than Angie's List.)

The same process can be used to determine if gluten and yeast over growth is a problem for you. Again, unfortunately, most physicians are not trained in detecting or treating gluten allergies or yeast over growth until it is a severe problem.

1. With the assistance of the weight ask, "Do I have an allergy to gluten?"
2. With the assistance of the weight ask, "Do I not have an allergy to gluten?"
3. If the response is positive ask, with the assistance of the weight, "Will performing the procedures defined in the Enlightenment process remove this gluten allergy?"
4. With the assistance of the weight, ask "Will performing the procedures defined in the Enlightenment process not remove this gluten allergy?"

Almost any allergy can be alleviated by removing the stored emotion that you, at some point in your life, associated with the substance you are allergic to.

5. With the assistance of the weight, ask "Would it be in the best interest of my health to stop ingesting gluten?"

6. With the assistance of the weight, ask "Would it not be in the best interest of my health to stop ingesting gluten?"

If the answer is positive, stop ingesting gluten until your Higher Self, through future inquiry from you, advises you that the allergy is no longer a problem for you.

Most contemporary diets contain large amounts of processed sugar and carbohydrates. This condition coupled with high instances of ingestion of meats laden with growth hormones and antibiotics, and the ingestion of antibiotics dispensed freely for the slightest discomfort facilitates the common affliction of yeast overgrowth. Once again it is difficult to detect yeast overgrowth with conventional medical testing until it reaches very advanced stages and is causing severe illness.

As with any unwanted condition, you can determine if these, or others conditions, are causing you difficulty by simply asking your Higher Self.

Prepare to talk to your Higher Self.

1. Close your eyes and keep them closed until you are finished with the session.
2. With the assistance of the weight, ask your Higher Self "Will you aid me in some physical diagnostic questions now?"
3. With the assistance of the weight, ask your Higher Self, "You will not aid me in some physical diagnostic questions now?"

If your Higher Self replies in the positive, then proceed.

4. With the assistance of the weight ask, "Do I have a yeast (Candida) overgrowth condition?"
5. With the assistance of the weight ask, "Do I not have a yeast (Candida) overgrowth condition?"
6. If the reply is positive, with the assistance of the weight ask, "Is this primarily caused by ingestion of sugar and/or carbohydrates?"
7. With the assistance of the weight ask, "Is this not primarily caused by ingestion of sugar and/or carbohydrates?"
8. With the assistance of the weight ask, "Is this primarily caused by ingestion of foods containing growth hormones and/or antibiotics?"
9. With the assistance of the weight ask, "Is this not primarily caused by ingestion of foods containing growth hormones and/or antibiotics?"
10. With the assistance of the weight ask, "Is this primarily caused by taking too many prescription antibiotics?"
11. With the assistance of the weight ask, "Is this not primarily caused by too many prescription antibiotics?"

Obviously, if the response is positive for things you are eating, you can change your diet immediately to remove all sugar and carbohydrates. You can also change your food selections to cease eating genetically modified organisms and eat only organically grown foods (without sugar).Finally, if antibiotics are a must for your health, you can locate a physician that can manage the antibiotic regimen with pro-biotic to balance the effects and side effects of the antibiotics. (You may also search for physicians that are trained to treat "Leaky Gut Syndrome".)

The last physical condition that we would like to address is drug usage, which includes alcohol usage. If you currently use drugs or alcohol to be entertained, or to smooth over the rough spots you will not be able to achieve Enlightenment. However, as you do the work as specified in the previous chapters, you will no longer need the drugs or alcohol. Actually, they will become undesirable because they will distract us from the good feeling/happiness that we are feeling all the time.

Drugs and/or alcohol are used to make us feel better. What makes us not feel good is the emotional baggage that we have stored within us. As we work to release the emotional baggage we no longer require something else to help us suppress these emotions.

We must be able to access the emotions comprising the emotional baggage. If we continue to try and mask these emotions with artificial substances we will only cause the persistence of the unpleasant feels that haunt us and dramatically slow the process of Enlightenment. Once again, we emphasis that when the pain of staying the same exceeds the pain of change, we will change. If the pain is great enough, you'll stop the divergent behavior and substances and begin to work to get rid of the root cause. Until then, you may not be ready. It's your choice.

This work is offered in the Love and the Light of the One Infinite Creator in the hope that you will awaken and, with the strength of your commitment, begin the work to heal yourself, achieve Enlightenment, and begin to experience true unity consciousness. Achieving Enlightenment is your right and the prize that is yours' alone to grasp.

Adonai vasu

Bibliography

Slavenski, Zivorad Mihajlovic, Phd.; **PEAT: New Pathways**, Belgrad, 2010. Zivorad Mihajlovic Slavenski, publisher.

Hawkins, David R., MD, Phd; **Power v Force: An Anatomy of Consciousness. The Hidden Determinants of Human Behavior.** Veritas Publishing, 1995.

Eden, Donna, and Feinstein, David, Phd.; **Energy Medicine. Balancing Your Body's Energies for Optimal Health, Joy, and Vitality.** Penguin Group, 1998, 2008.

Rassmussen, George, and Ducharme, Robert; **Personal Interviews.** Memphis, TN.

Daniel, Judith; **Personal Interviews.** Louisville, KY.

Tolle, Eckhart; **The Power of Now: a guide to spiritual enlightenment.** New World Library, Novato, CA and Namaste Publishing, Vancouver, B.C., 1999.